Bible Acrostic Code Mysteries

Revealing DNA, Fractal and Quantum Creative Linguistics

Carl Armstrong and Mark & Cathy Eaton

Mark and Cathy Eaton
972-248-5078
bridgeinggap@gmail.com
lovewhoyouare@gmail.com

BIBLE ACROSTIC CODE MYSTERIES
by Carl Armstrong and Mark & Cathy Eaton
Published by: *Dallas & DaySpring Publishers*

This book or parts thereof may not be reproduced in any form, stored in a retrieval system, or transmitted in any form by any means— electronic, mechanical, photocopy, recording, or otherwise—without prior written permission of the publisher, except as provided by United States of America copyright law.

Unless otherwise noted, all Scripture quotations are from the King James Version of the Bible. Bolding of selected words or phrases has been added by the authors for purposes of emphasis.

The authors have made every effort to provide citations for information accessed from the internet and their corresponding web addresses. Neither the publisher nor the authors assume any responsibility for changes made in web addresses or their contents that occur after the access dates given in this publication.

First edition

Copyright © 2016 Carl Armstrong and Mark & Cathy Eaton

All rights reserved.

ISBN-13: 978-1536844924
ISBN-10: 1536844926

DEDICATION

TO THE SON OF THE HIGHEST

He shall be great, and shall be called the Son of the Highest:
and the Lord God shall give unto him the throne of his father David:
And he shall reign over the house of Jacob for ever; and of his
kingdom there shall be no end.

LUKE 1:32-33

CONTENTS

	Introduction	i
1	If We Could Only Witness Creation's Beginning	1
2	From Darkness into Light	4
3	A Rod of an Almond Tree	9
4	Scientists "Discover" Seven Hidden Dimensions	13
5	The Acrostic Pattern for DNA	20
6	The DNA and RNA Codes	25
7	The Twenty-two Letter Protein Building Code	29
8	Chromosomes and Genes	32
9	Acrostics in Proverbs, Psalms and Lamentations	40
10	The Roots of the Hebrew Language	45
11	The Body of Christ Working Together	50
12	Psalms Nine Plus Psalms Ten Acrostics	53
13	The Psalm Chapter 25 Acrostic	58
14	The Psalm Chapter 34 Acrostic	61
15	The Psalm Chapter 37 Acrostic	64
16	The Psalms Chapters 111 & 112 Acrostic	68
17	Opening the Psalm 119 Matrix	71
18	The Psalm 145 Acrostic	76
19	Lamentations Acrostics	79
20	The Esther Acrostic	85
21	From Nahum's Acrostic to Telepathy	88
22	Summarizing the Patterns	93
	APPENDIX: Treasures of Science in the Bible	98

INTRODUCTION

There is always an excitement of adventure as we explore the unknown. Those that sailed the vast Atlantic to the "New World" brought back wondrous stories of peoples and lands. Those that ventured into space for the first time and even set foot on the moon captured the imagination of earth's people.

Ride along with us as we journey through the largely unexplored land of Bible acrostics. Yes, these acrostic verses with lines that have words in a pre-arranged alphabetical pattern have their own beauty as prose and poetry. Many Bible scholars have acknowledged and appreciated that over the years and centuries. But further exploration reveals these acrostics have a coded pattern in which mysteries of DNA, fractals, hidden dimensions and quantum mechanics are revealed. Are the modern 'discoveries' of science uncovering what was already embedded in scriptures from ancient times?

> It is the glory of God to conceal a thing:
> but the honour of kings is to search out a matter.
> PROVERBS 25:2

1 IF WE COULD ONLY WITNESS CREATION'S BEGINNING

A viewer emailed this question to the TV panel: If you could go back in time and watch any historical event, what event would you choose? The answers were varied and a few chose more recent events. However, three of the panel having a Christian background chose the following: 1. Jesus being resurrected and the stone being rolled away from the tomb 2. The miracle of the loaves and fishes. The third member wished to see chaos being dispelled when the words, "Let there be Light." were spoken.

Given our English (or other language background) would we understand the creative words being spoken—were they spoken in Hebrew? Since the Hebrews were deemed by the Lord as a *peculiar treasure unto me above all people* and a *royal priesthood*, it would be highly probable the creative words were spoken in Hebrew.

There is a particular modern mindset that the ancients (including God—if even existing) knew very little about science and this lack of understanding is reflected in the scriptures. However, the flip side of that argument is that God would have to had a profound understanding of quantum physics, hidden dimensions and DNA in order to have created the world. Is it possible that man is just beginning to discover what God knew all along from the beginning of creation? A king named Solomon made these observations:

ECCLESIASTES 1:9 The thing that hath been, it is that which shall be; and that which is done is that which shall be done: and **there is no new thing under the sun**.
10 Is there any thing whereof it may be said, See, this is new? it hath been already of old time, which was before us.

This is a startling way of looking at creation. The scripture doesn't say no new thing exists in the universe, but it does confine it to this solar system of which even Voyager is struggling to find its outer boundaries. When one looks at discoveries and inventions, it is not unusual for those separated by geography to independently arrive at the Eureka! moment almost simultaneously—as if something were being unsealed for mankind via a master timing program.

A senior scientist at Southwest Research, upon being assigned a new project, gave this thought-provoking advice for his team: " First, we look at how nature does it. Often, we can follow the lead of nature and come up with a much better solution than what has been attempted in the past." The validity of this approach can be seen in the wonders of nature. Bats have a built-in sonar. Dogs have a sense of smell that puts to shame many modern analytical instruments. Migratory birds 'somehow' have a sense of routes that is still not quite understood. Chameleons have invisibility cloaking that is being studied by modern scientists. And the list goes on and on.

Those that have explored the mysteries of the right and left brain speak of a division between intuitive creative thinking and logical, mental reasoning. In both Hebrew and secular history, there often existed a breach between the king and the priest. And, this has carried down to the present day in the schism between politics and religion—or for that matter, between 'science' and spirituality.

Where are we going with all this? Scientists of the post-Einstein era have earnestly been exploring seven 'hidden' dimensions. Their thinking is in addition to the very familiar dimensions of our natural *under the sun* world (length, width, depth and time) there are seven so-called hidden dimensions—making a total of eleven dimensions. Is it possible for the stroke of non-communication between the left brained—under the natural sun world—and the right brained spiritual world to be healed? Does this have anything to do with the illumination provided by the seven Spirits of God? Maybe—we read from the scripture:

ISAIAH 30:26 Moreover the light of the moon shall be as the light of the sun, **and the light of the sun shall be sevenfold**, as the light of seven days, in the day that **the LORD bindeth up the breach of his people, and healeth the stroke of their wound.**

In this book, we will explore the use of Bible acrostics that provide a structure for the twenty-two letters of the Hebrew alphabet. An acrostic is a structured linguistic that alphabetically normally uses the first position in the first word of a series of sentences—for example, a four letter acrostic.

Apples are a tasty fruit.
Bees pollinate flowers.
Camels travel the deserts.
Doors often have locks.

Yes, doors have locks, but locks have keys and opening those sealed doors can reveal mysteries. But first things first. If you are skeptical that treasures of science hidden in the pages of the Bible are being discovered, we suggest that you skip to page 98 for a section entitled *Treasures of Science in the Bible*. This lists a plethora of examples—many of which are just being 'discovered' by scientists today. Then come back to this point in chapter 1.

There are so many examples of embedded scientific gems in the Bible; however in this book we want to confine our main focus to acrostics involved in creation. Otherwise, we will be distracted by chasing too many other subjects while on the trail of creation mysteries.

So, where does this trail start and where is it leading? Let's do an eagle's eye overflight of the terrain. It begins with "Let there be light." Where does light come from symbolically? It comes from the seven lamped candlestick. What is unique about the candlestick?—in its structure it has twenty-two embedded symbols which is the same number as the Hebrew alphabet. Where is the Hebrew alphabet **frame** presented in acrostic form in the Bible?—in Psalms 119 and many other places.

HEBREWS 11:3 Through faith we understand that the **worlds were framed by the word of God**, so that things which are seen were not made of things which do appear.

If we could only watch creation's beginning. Job, after complaining about all his trials and tribulations, was caught up in the time warp of the Lord's whirlwind and was asked these questions:

JOB 38:1 Then the LORD answered Job out of the whirlwind, and said,
…
4 **Where wast thou when I laid the foundations of the earth**? declare, if thou hast understanding.
5 Who hath laid the measures thereof, if thou knowest? or who hath stretched the line upon it?
6 Whereupon are the foundations thereof fastened? or who laid the corner stone thereof;
7 **When the morning stars sang together, and all the sons of God shouted for joy?**

2 FROM DARKNESS INTO LIGHT

We will begin with the lifting of the chaotic darkness as described in Genesis 1:3

ג וַיֹּאמֶר אֱלֹהִים, יְהִי אוֹר; וַיְהִי-אוֹר. **3** And God said: 'Let there be light.' And there was light.

If you can read Hebrew—very good. You know that you read Hebrew from right to left; while English is read from left to right. However, for most of us, looking at the Hebrew characters brings back memories of our kindergarten or first grade primer experiences. But, like in English, each character is a building block used to form a word and a word is a symbol which represents a reality or a thought.

So we will start with the Hebrew word אוֹר (light) and relate it to another Hebrew word מְנֹרַת (candlestick or alternately translated lampstand). In the wilderness, Moses was given very precise instructions on how to build a tabernacle or tent which housed among other furnishings a lampstand. A lampstand in full utilization symbolizes the olive oil of the Holy Spirit flowing into the word framework of the lampstand and ignited/lighted by the Spirit to give light.

GENESIS 1:2 And the earth was without form, and void; and darkness was upon the face of the deep. And the **Spirit of God moved** upon the face of the waters.
3 And God **said**, Let there be **light**: and there was **light.**

HEBREWS 11:3 Through faith we understand that **the worlds were framed by the word of God**, so that things which are seen were not made of things which do appear.

Now that we have defined the light in Genesis and related it to words that God said, what does this candlestick framework for words look like?

EXODUS 25:31 And thou shalt make a candlestick of pure gold: of beaten work shall the candlestick be made: his shaft, and his branches, his bowls, his knops, and his flowers, shall be of the same.

Fig 2.1 Artist's depiction of the Hebrew candlestick

We now have a 'visual' of the candlestick, we will continue with the blueprint given to Moses for its construction. We can see it has seven lamps and engraved work like some kind of flowers embedded in the shaft. But, here's a challenge for you—can you decipher the embedded code as related to the Hebrew alphabet in the candlestick's construction.

EXO 25:32 And **six branches** shall come out of the sides of it; **three branches of the candlestick out of the one side, and three branches of the candlestick out of the other side**:
33 Three bowls **made like unto almonds**, with a knop and a flower in one branch; and three bowls made like almonds in the other branch, with a knop and a flower: **so in the six branches that come out of the candlestick.**
34 **And in the candlestick shall be four bowls made like unto almonds**, with their knops and their flowers.
35 And there shall be a knop under two branches of the same, and a knop under two branches of the same, and a knop under two branches of the same, according to the six branches that proceed out of the candlestick.
36 Their knops and their branches shall be of the same: all it shall be one beaten work of pure gold.
37 **And thou shalt make the seven lamps thereof: and they shall light the lamps** thereof, that they may give light over against it.

Maybe this is sort of like the game of 'hot and cold'. But here are a few hints. Count how many almond flowers are on each branch of the candlestick and then multiply it by the number of branches. Then, add to that number the sum of the almond flowers in the main candlestick shaft—and what number do you get? Could this number be related to the Hebrew alphabet?

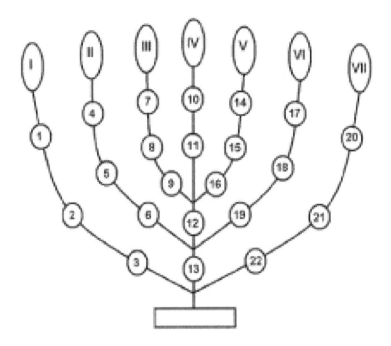

Fig. 2.2 Numbering the lamps and almond flowers in the Hebrew candlestick

If you came up with twenty-two almond flowers—very good. But what does this number have to do with the Hebrew alphabet? If you turn in your Bible to Psalm 119, you will find it is arranged in eight verse sets. **The first eight verses begin with the Hebrew letter Aleph**, and the **next eight begin with the letter Beth** and so on until you reach **the final and twenty-second letter taw.** Psalms 119 is the master, acrostic list of the Hebrew letters in the Bible.

PSALMS 119   ALEPH
1 Blessed are the undefiled in the way, who walk in the law of the LORD.
2 Blessed are they that keep his testimonies, and that seek him with the whole heart.
3 They also do no iniquity: they walk in his ways.
4 Thou hast commanded us to keep thy precepts diligently.
5 O that my ways were directed to keep thy statutes!
6 Then shall I not be ashamed, when I have respect unto all thy commandments.
7 I will praise thee with uprightness of heart, when I shall have learned thy righteous judgments.
8 I will keep thy statutes: O forsake me not utterly.

               BETH
9 Wherewithal shall a young man cleanse his way? by taking heed thereto according to thy word. ...
               TAW
169 Let my cry come near before thee ...

176 I have gone astray like a lost sheep, seek thy servant; for I do not forget thy commandments.

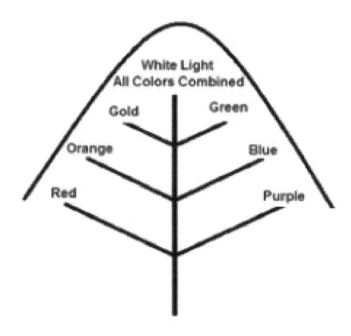

Fig. 2.3 The spectrum of natural light visible to the human eye

As it is true with sound, light comes in octaves. Below our perceptive vision is an octave ending with infrared and above is an octave beginning with ultra-violet. A full range piano has eleven octaves. Is it co-incidence that the Psalm 119 acrostic is arranged in sets of eight verses.

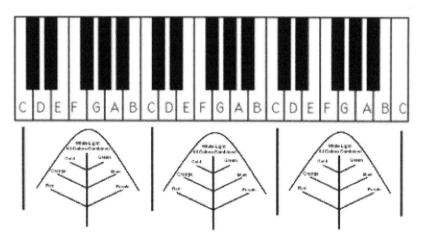

Fig. 2.4 Octaves of sound and light

Now, a reasonable question to ask is why the candlestick has seven lamps. We often speak of the Holy Spirit or perhaps in the Old Testament, the Spirit of God. Yes, the Holy Spirit is one unified Spirit, but it has seven dimensions—just as represented in the candlestick. Perhaps that knowledge is a bit hidden, but it becomes very clear when we examine the following scriptures.

REVELATION 4:5 And out of the throne proceeded **lightnings** and thunderings and voices: and there were **seven lamps of fire** burning before the throne, which are the **seven Spirits of God**.

ISAIAH 11:1 And **there shall come forth a rod** out of the stem of Jesse, and a **Branch** shall grow out of his roots:
2 And the **spirit of the LORD** shall rest upon him, the spirit of **wisdom** and **understanding**, the spirit of **counsel** and **might**, the spirit of **knowledge** and of **the fear of the LORD**;

What are the names of the seven Spirits of God. They are named in Isaiah 11:2: The main white light shaft of the candlestick is *1.* ***Spirit of the Lord****.* Following are *2.* ***Wisdom*** *3.* ***Understanding*** *4.* ***Counsel*** *5. Might 6.* ***Knowledge*** *and 7.* ***Fear of the Lord****.*

Now there is one other notable feature of the candlestick and that is the rod as outlined in Isaiah 11:1. What kind of rod? It is an almond rod and did we not read that the candlestick has twenty-two almond flowers on its branches and shaft.?

The almond rod is used mightily in the Old Testament to bring deliverance to the Israelites. However, most people do not realize that it was an almond rod—instead they just think of it as the rod of Moses. The almond rod is the subject of the next chapter.

3 A ROD OF AN ALMOND TREE

JEREMIAH 1:11 Moreover the word of the LORD came unto me, saying, Jeremiah, what seest thou? And I said, I see **a rod of an almond tree**.
12 Then said the LORD unto me, Thou hast well seen: for **I will hasten my word to perform it.**

The above scripture truly relates the relationship between the symbol of the almond rod and the spoken word of God—perhaps in a place where we did not expect it. However, the rod of Moses was used in the performance of many miracles for deliverance of the Hebrews and we will begin there where it is first mentioned in the Bible.

EXODUS 3:2 And the angel of the LORD appeared unto him in a flame of fire out of the midst of a bush: and he looked, and, behold, the bush burned with fire, and the bush was not consumed. …
EXODUS 4:1 And Moses answered and said, But, behold, they will not believe me, nor hearken unto my voice: for they will say, The LORD hath not appeared unto thee.
2 And the LORD said unto him, **What is that in thine hand? And he said, A rod.**
…
EXODUS 4:14 And the anger of the LORD was kindled against Moses, and he said**, Is not Aaron the Levite thy brother?** I know that he can speak well. And also, behold, he cometh forth to meet thee: and when he seeth thee, he will be glad in his heart.
15 **And thou shalt speak unto him, and put words in his mouth:** and I will be with thy mouth, and with his mouth, and will teach you what ye shall do.
16 And **he shall be thy spokesman unto the people**: and he shall be, even **he shall be to thee instead of a mouth**, and thou shalt be to him instead of God.
17 **And thou shalt take this rod in thine hand, wherewith thou shalt do signs.**

OK, fine, we all know about the miracles that Moses and Aaron did in Egypt and also in the wilderness. But how do we know that rod was an almond rod? Well, were not Moses and Aaron brothers in the priesthood tribe of Levi?

NUMBERS 17:7 And Moses laid up **the rods before the LORD** in the tabernacle of witness.

8 And it came to pass, that on the morrow Moses went into the tabernacle of witness; and, behold, **the rod of Aaron for the house of Levi was budded, and brought forth buds, and bloomed blossoms, and yielded almonds**.

So, this rod was used in all the miracles performed in Egypt, the parting of the Red Sea, the striking of the rock to provide water and the provision of manna. However, there is a history of this rod that was already in Moses' hand when he ascended the mountain to observe the burning bush. There are two references in the Bible to what is *written in the book of Jasher*. See Joshua 10:13 and 2 Samuel 1:18. The book of Jasher (chapter 77) may be referenced online at http://www.sacred-texts.com/chr/apo/jasher/77.htm and the rod is first mentioned in verse 39. And the book of Jasher details its history all the way back to God's creative words in Genesis.

Fig 3.1 Artist's depiction of Aaron's rod that budded.

In Chapter 6, we will delve into the DNA codes. However, it does appear that the almond rod is involved in DNA replication. Sometimes nuggets are hidden in translations other the KJV and we run across a mention of the almond rod in the NIV. The context is of Jacob altering the bovine hair hide color—part of DNA coding--so he could have his own 'brand' of cattle separate from his father-in-law Laban

GENESIS 30: **37** Jacob, however, took fresh-cut branches from **poplar, almond** and **plane** trees and made white stripes on them by **peeling the bark and exposing the white inner wood of the branches**. **38** Then he placed the peeled branches in all the watering troughs, so that they would be directly in front of the flocks when they came to drink. When the flocks were in heat and came to drink, **39 they mated in front of the branches**. And they bore young that were streaked or speckled or spotted. **40** Jacob set apart the young of the flock by themselves, but made the rest face the streaked and dark-colored animals that belonged to Laban. Thus he made separate flocks for himself and did not put them with Laban's animals. (NIV)

We might scoff at this story and say that Jacob's tribe could not possibly have understood DNA technology, and if they did, it was only the basic concepts of selective breeding. Surely, Jacob did not understand how the RNA helix is peeled open in order to make a DNA copy as the cells reproduce themselves by dividing—or possibly did a 'higher power' provide the technology used to create the world as a favor to Jacob? The KJV translates the "branches" in the above verses as rods. Another Bible scripture that relates rods to genetics is as follows:

EZEKIEL 19:10 Thy mother is like a **vine in thy blood**, planted by the waters: **she was fruitful and full of branches by reason of many waters**.
11 And she had **strong rods for the sceptres of them that bare rule**, and her stature was exalted among the thick branches, and she appeared in her height with the multitude of her branches.
12 But she was plucked up in fury, she was cast down to the ground, and the east wind dried up her fruit: **her strong rods were broken and withered; the fire consumed them.**
13 And now she is planted in the wilderness, in a dry and thirsty ground.
14 **And fire is gone out of a rod of her branches,** which hath devoured her fruit, so that **she hath no strong rod to be a sceptre** to rule. **This is a lamentation**, and shall be for a lamentation.

We can look at some of the symbols in the above verses. The DNA spiral has a **vine** like configuration and the Bible tells us the *life of the flesh is in the blood*. The **branches** or the **rods** are involved in the mitosis or the division of cells. The **rods** are sometimes called **spindles** and are actually what is known as microtubules. Microtubules are hollow 'wave guides' for transmitting information—somewhat similar to the fiber optic technology used in phone systems.

The procedure that Jacob used involved three branches or rods, not just two as we commonly think of in regarding the DNA spiraling vine configuration. The three rods listed are the **poplar**, **almond and plane** rods. Scientists have been fervently working with the two spirals of DNA. They can splice in genes and can even clone dogs, cats, sheep and probably are attempting covertly to clone people. They have run into one major problem in that they can 'copycat' life **given an original seed**, but they can't find the **original spark** of life to jump start the synthetic compounds they make. So, we will make a hypothesis here and our readers can be the judge.

JOHN 1:9 That was the true Light, which **lighteth every man** that cometh into the world.

We have discussed the almond bud candlestick symbolism as the bearer of the light of the spoken word: *Let there be light.* There is a divine spark within each of us and within everything that has life. DNA has two 'seen' spiral rails with ladder rungs between—does it have an unseen third rail? Now, think of a metropolitan railway system with its two rails and the ties supporting them.

Fig. 3.2 Metropolitan rail system with third rail energy source

Without the third rail energy source, the engine and its cars would be dead on the track. The almond rod may be the symbol of a third rail life source within the DNA vine, and yet is not seen in the natural world by investigating scientists. *Through faith we understand that the worlds were framed by the word of God, so that things which are seen were not made of things which do appear.*

ECCLESIASTES 12:6 **Or ever the silver cord be loosed**, or the golden bowl be broken, or the pitcher be broken at the fountain, or the wheel broken at the cistern.
7 Then shall the dust return to the earth as it was: and **the spirit shall return unto God who gave it.**

So, you be the judge—is there a third unseen 'rail' that is present in the DNA spiral and also in the rods that are peeled?

The very issues of life flow from God's Spirit. We can begin to understand how *there shall come forth a rod out of the stem of Jesse* which symbolizes the seven Spirits of God—and further how the seven lamped Hebrew lampstand is embedded with the twenty-two almond buds represents the power of the spoken word of the twenty-two characters of the Hebrew alphabet. We will later examine how multiples and half-multiples of the twenty-two letters show up in nature and curiously are even embedded in the mysterious mathematical pi. However, we want to first examine the **seven hidden dimensions of the Spirit of God**.

4 SCIENTISTS 'DISCOVER' SEVEN HIDDEN DIMENSIONS

JOHN 3:8 The wind bloweth where it listeth, and thou hearest the sound thereof, but canst not tell whence it cometh, and whither it goeth: so is every one that is born of the Spirit.

Earlier, in chapter 1, we touched on the four normal dimensions that we encounter in everyday life. And then we alluded to seven additional, hidden dimensions which are being studied by the scientists. Let's further define the four 'seen' dimensions.

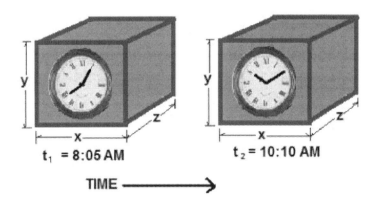

Fig. 4.1 The four dimensions under the sun of the natural world

Think of a clock installed within a block of wood. The block of wood has length (x), height (y), depth (z) and at time (t_1) we observe it at 8:05 a.m. A little later, the dimensions of the block of wood have not perceptibly changed, but two hours and five minutes have passed in the time dimension for our observation made at time t_2. So far, this is familiar to us. But what could these hidden dimensions be that scientists have very recently considered?

Remember that Moses went up on the mountain to view the burning bush and it was also on the mountain where he was given the pattern for the tabernacle including the candlestick.

EXODUS 24:15 And **Moses went up into the mount**, and a cloud covered the mount. … 25:9 According to all that I shew thee, after the pattern of the tabernacle, and **the pattern of all the instruments thereof,** even so shall ye make it.

Here is the account of a journey to a mountaintop recent discovery by scientists as it was given on the Science Channel. This was a BBC/Horizon production entitled *Parallel Universes*. The speakers in the transcribed dialog are the narrator and also professors Michael Duff (University of Michigan; Imperial College London), Burt Ovrut (University of Pennsylvania), Michio Kaku (City College of NY), and Paul Steinhardt (Princeton University).

Sometimes the words quantum physics, hidden dimensions and/or related string theory invoke "I don't or won't understand it reactions." However, if you are non-technical, please don't get bogged down in the technical terms—just look at the final conclusion which reveals the pattern.

The following presentation describes an academic struggle—or almost warfare—between two camps of physicists that occurred around the turn of century. In one camp the **String Theory** physicists, who likened matter to vibrating strings, found their equations were convincing them that **ten total dimensions existed.**

A smaller group of physicists led by University of Michigan professor Michael Duff proposed the **Supergravity Theory** and **insisted** that **eleven dimensions existed**. For a while string theory was in ascendancy and then serious doubts arose **when string theory splintered into five competing theories**. And here are some brief excerpts from the program *Parallel Universes* describing how the string theory and supergravity combatants finally made peace. It starts with a comment from Michael Duff, the proponent of **Supergravity**.

So, here is the excerpted narrative from ***Parallel Universes*** as presented on the Science Channel.

"**DUFF:** The equations of super gravity took the simplest and most elegant form when written in this eleven-dimensional framework.

KAKU: There was a war between the tenth dimension and the eleventh dimension….

NARRATOR: In a final desperate move, the string theorists tried adding one last thing to their cherished idea. They added the very thing they had spent a decade rubbishing: the eleventh dimension. Now something almost magical happened to the five competing theories.

OVRUT: The answer turned out to be remarkable—and it was really absolutely remarkable, it turns out they were the same! These five string theories turned out to be simply different manifestations of a more fundamental theory.

KAKU: In eleven dimensions—looking from the mountain top—looking down you could see string theory as being part of a much larger reality—the reality of the eleventh dimension....

NARRATOR: The two camps had been absolutely certain the other was wrong. Now, suddenly, they realized their ideas complimented each other perfectly. With the addition of one extra dimension, string theory made sense again. But, it had become a very different kind of theory.

OVRUT: What happened to the string?

NARRATOR: The tiny invisible strings of string theory were supposed to be the fundamental building blocks of the matter in the universe. But now, with the addition of the eleventh dimension, they changed. They stretched and combined. The astonishing conclusion as that all the mater in the universe was connected to one membrane. In effect, our entire universe is a membrane. The quest to explain everything in the universe would begin again and its heart would be this new theory. It was dubbed M-theory or Membrane theory."

****

IN CONCLUSION: A leading scientist states: "In eleven dimensions—looking from the mountaintop—looking down you could see string theory as being part of a much larger reality—the reality of the eleventh dimension."

On the mountain Moses was told about the furnishings of the tabernacle in the wilderness: "Who serve unto the example and **shadow of heavenly** things, as Moses was admonished of God when he was about to make the tabernacle: for, See, saith he, that thou make all things **according to the pattern shewed to thee in the mount.**"

Isn't it interesting, and perhaps even astounding, that scientists are discovering that adding the four **seen** dimensions to the seven **unseen** dimensions of the Spirit, we get a total of eleven dimensions? Eleven is a half-multiple of the twenty-two letters of the Hebrew alphabet. What treasures will we find with a full multiple or a double multiple of the twenty-two letters?

HEBREWS 11:1 Now faith is the substance of things hoped for, the evidence of **things not seen**. ...
3 Through faith we understand that the worlds were framed by the word of God, **so that things which are seen were not made of things which do appear.**

And, as a bonus from the above discussion, the scientists are considering the entire universe to be a membrane. A membrane is stretchable and the number of scriptures in the Bible about God stretching out the world is amazing. Here is just one of them.

JEREMIAH 10:12 He hath made the earth by his power, he hath established the world by his wisdom, and **hath stretched out the heavens by his discretion.**

And, at this point, we will add just a little reinforcement to the idea that the universe may be symbolized by eleven dimensions as part of a stretchable membrane. Physicist Brian Greene of Columbia University describes the work of cutting-edge string theorist Edward Witten in his recent book *The Fabric of the Cosmos* as follows:

"Eleven Dimensions

So, with our newfound power to analyze string theory, what insights have emerged? There have been many. I will focus on those that have had the greatest impact on the story of space and time.

Of primary importance, Witten's work revealed that the approximate string theory equations used in the 1970s and 1980s to conclude that universe must have nine space dimensions missed the true number by one. The exact answer, his analysis showed, is that the universe according to M-theory has ten space dimensions, that is, eleven spacetime dimensions. Much as Kaluza found that a universe with five spacetime dimensions proved a framework for unifying electromagnetism and gravity, and much as string theorists found that a universe with ten spacetime dimensions provided a framework for unifying quantum mechanics and general relativity, Witten found that a universe with eleven spacetime dimensions provided a framework for unifying, all string theories.

. . . While Witten's discovery surely fit the historical pattern of achieving unity through more dimensions, when he announced the result at the annual international string theory conference in 1995, it shook the foundations of the field." (p. 383, *The Fabric of the Cosmos* by Brian Greene).

ISAIAH 40:22 It is he that sitteth upon **the circle of the earth**, and the inhabitants thereof are as grasshoppers; **that stretcheth out the heavens as a curtain**, and spreadeth them out as a tent to dwell in:

Could it be that the Lord also knew the earth was circular in shape—in spite of some of mankind's 'flat earth' theories?

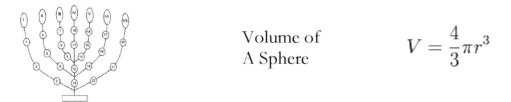

Volume of A Sphere $V = \dfrac{4}{3}\pi r^3$

Fig. 4.2 The candlestick with 22 almond knops and seven lamps; Pi. in the sphere formula

Now there is another unusual feature of the eleven dimensions in creation, but in this case related to fractals—a way of nature having a 'cookie cutter' which replicates itself—more about this later. Remember the configuration of the candlestick with its 22 almond knops. and seven lamps? How could this be related to one of the fundamental constants of nature which is known as Pi and is often rounded off to 3.14. Uniquely enough, when we take the number 22 and divide it by 7 we get 3.14. Perhaps just co-incidence, but let's pursue it further.

So, we compare the 22/7 result with the actual number for π. As the mathematicians among you know, Pi is an unending number that can be computed as long as someone wants to put in the effort to do it—and then on to forever and forever. Here is the comparison.

22/7 =   3.14285714285714000000000000000

π =   3.1415926535 8979323846 264338327 ...

The number is quite close, but slightly different, as if there is a certain differential between the seen and the unseen. We have discussed the multiples of eleven in language and DNA. Could there be multiples of eleven encoded in π?

3.14159265358979323846264**33**8327950２**88**41971693**99**375105820974**44**592 307816406286208**99**862803482534211**11**706798214808651328230**66**470938**446** 09**55**058**22**31725359408128481**11**7450284102701938521**1**0**55**596**446**22**9**489 54930381964428109756659**3344**61284756482**33**7867831652712019091456**48** 5**66**923460348610543**266**48213**3**93607260249141273724587006 ...

Pi is related to going in circles and circles can repeat themselves by going in the same racetrack that was the path of the original circle. Think of the three dimensional spirals of DNA—which viewed from the top in two dimensions look like just one circle. And this is also true of fractals which are nature's way of duplication from an original pattern in three dimensions. So, let's briefly consider fractals.

You might think of a fractal as something that reproduces itself over and over again. You could think of a cooking cutter stamping out a shape of dough. Then the extremely virile yeast in this dough expands growing more little cookie cutter shapes of itself which grow into more cookie cutter offspring, etc., etc.

Fig. 4.3 A reproducing fractal compared to the Hebrew candlestick

Notice in the fractal diagram on the left how the big circular shape has smaller circular shapes growing out of it which in turn has little, bitty circular shapes growing out of them. Why is this important? It is one of the fundamental ways that nature reproduces itself by using the same simple pattern over and over to produce amazingly complex shapes and structures.

Benoit Mandelbrot, an IBM employee and later a Yale professor, astonished his colleagues in 1975 by publishing a book called *The Fractal Geometry of Nature*. The book espoused what is known as chaos theory. This theory took very complex systems of nature such as snowflakes, cell division, circulatory system branching, shorelines, patterns of flights of birds and numerous other patterns and related them to a simple, repeating equation.

The equation uses the concept of feedback. An example is a microphone that picks up the amplified sound from a speaker and feeds it back on itself. All of us have experienced the high frequency screeeeeeee… that makes one hold their ears as the frequency goes out the roof. Or, another example might be a camera that sends a signal to a video screen that the camera is filming. Strange, beautiful and complex patterns may develop after a period of time that bear little resemblance to the camera or the video screen.

A well-known description of how a small change which feeds back on itself and produces the huge effect of fractals reproducing themselves is one of the classic titles and questions of chaos theory: *Does the flap of a butterfly's wings in Brazil set off a tornado in Texas?* The idea is that the energy from the flap of the butterfly's wings feeds back and feeds back over and over until it has reached gigantic proportions in a Texas storm.

The most fascinating part is how very complex and seemingly chaotic systems are regulated by a disarmingly simple form of a feedback equation. Here it is:

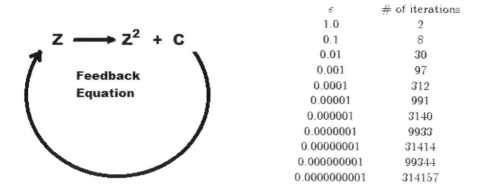

ε	# of iterations
1.0	2
0.1	8
0.01	30
0.001	97
0.0001	312
0.00001	991
0.000001	3140
0.0000001	9933
0.00000001	31414
0.000000001	99344
0.0000000001	314157

Fig. 4.4 Illustration of feedback formula and Boll's number of iterations to reach π

Anything going in a circle is likely to involve π. The occurrence of π in Mandelbrot sets was developed by David Boll and discussed in *The World of π* website[1]. He calculated how many circles of growth **a daughter Mandelbrot figure** would have to iterate **before it achieved escape from its mother figure.** Strangely, that number correlates with 3.14157 or π and requires **eleven sets of iterations**. An amazing co-incidence in nature's (and by the way, God's) creation.

That is why we are so fascinated by **the multiples of eleven** in both the hidden dimensions of the universe and the Mandelbrot π series of numbers. The Hebrew candlestick pattern seems to be the underlying template of creation.

5 THE ACROSTIC PATTERN FOR DNA

THE CHARACTERS AND THEIR PICTURE-IMAGES			
Character		Name	Original Picture Symbolism
א		'Aleph	ox head, yoke, learn
ב		Beth	house, tent
ג		Gimel	camel's neck, soul
ד		Dâleth	door, curtain to tent
ה		Hê	window, lattice
ו		Wâw or vâv	hook, nail, peg
ז		Zayin	weapon
ח		Cheth	hedge, fence, surround, gird
ט		Teth	serpent, snake, roll, curve
י		Yodh	hand (bent)
כ	ך	Kaph	wing, palm (hollow of the hand)
ל		Lâmedh	ox goad, correction, learning
מ	ם	Mem	waves, water
נ	ן	Nun	fish (tadpole?), snake
ס		Sâmekh	prop, support
ע		'Ayin	eye
פ	ף	Pê	mouth
צ	ץ	Tsâdhe	fish hook? tool for cutting down?
ק		Qoph	axe, monkey, back of the head
ר		Resh	head
שׂ שׁ		Sin, Shin	tooth
ת		Tâw	sign, branded cross, mark, 'T'

Fig. 5.1 A pictorial representation of the twenty-two letters of the Hebrew alphabet
BiblicalHebrew.com, "Alphabet," http://biblicalhebrew.com/alphabet.htm. (accessed 6/22/16)[2]

Let's go back to the garden and look at Adam's beginning.

GENESIS 2:7 And the LORD God formed man of the dust of the ground, and breathed into his nostrils the breath of life; and **man became a living soul**.

GENESIS 2:21 And the LORD God caused a deep sleep to fall upon Adam, and he slept: and he took one of his ribs, and closed up the flesh instead thereof;
22 **And the rib, which the LORD God had taken from man, made he a woman**, and brought her unto the man.
23 And Adam said, This is now bone of my bones, and flesh of my flesh: she shall be called Woman, because she was taken out of Man.
24 Therefore shall a **man** leave his father and his mother, and shall cleave unto his **wife**: and they shall be one flesh.

Now, here is a question. In Genesis 2:7, was the DNA of Adam male or was it female? And yet, in verses 21 through 23, it becomes clear that the DNA of Adam was differentiated by the chromosomes which define the sex of the human. We understand that that we receive part of our DNA chromosomes from our mother and an equal amount of DNA chromosomes from our father. So, let's look at a representation of male DNA.

Chromosome Diagram for Male Human

XWWWWWWWWWWWWWWWWWWWWWW-----MMMMMMMMMMMMMMMMMMMMMM Y

23 Chromosomes from mother/Woman **(W)**   23 Chromosomes from father/male **(M)**

The diagram symbolically shows a male human's DNA which received 23 chromosomes from the mother—note the 23rd X chromosome on the left hand side. The male received 23 chromosomes from his father and the 23rd Y chromosome on the right resulted in the male being a male. However, if the father's sperm had contributed twenty-three chromosomes with an X chromosome at the end, he would have had a daughter—as shown below.

XWWWWWWWWWWWWWWWWWWWWWW-----MMMMMMMMMMMMMMMMMMMMMMX

Now mankind has a total of 23 + 23 chromosomes giving a total of 46 chromosomes in the DNA nucleus. However, the 23rd chromosome on each wing of the DNA nucleus is that which determines sex. Scientists have a name for the **remaining twenty-two non-sex determining chromosomes**, they are called **autosomes** and each human has a total of **forty-four autosomes** in the DNA nucleus.

Given this introduction, we have the table set in order to begin our investigation between the twenty-two letter acrostic in Psalm 119 and the pattern of DNA as revealed in the human autosomes. First, some basic information. You are familiar with the double spiral configuration of DNA and probably know the connectors between the two spirals are four types of molecules. One connector couple is A and T. Another connector couple is G and C. Obviously, we have used shorthand to describe some complex molecules, but at this point, we are just providing an overview.

EXODUS 25:40 And look that thou make them after their **pattern**, which was shewed thee in the mount.

Moses was told to follow a pattern which was shown him. So, let's search for a pattern within the twenty-two letter acrostic within Psalm 119 and compare it to the pattern for DNA.

PSALMS 119

Verses begins with ALEPH א

1 Blessed are the undefiled in the way, who walk in the law of the LORD.
2 Blessed are they that keep his testimonies, and that seek him with the whole heart.
3 They also do no iniquity: they walk in his ways.
4 Thou hast commanded us to keep thy precepts diligently.
5 O that my ways were directed to keep thy statutes!
6 Then shall I not be ashamed, when I have respect unto all thy commandments.
7 I will praise thee with uprightness of heart, when I shall have learned thy righteous judgments.
8 I will keep thy statutes: O forsake me not utterly.

Verses begins with BETH ב

9 Wherewithal shall a young man cleanse his way? by taking heed thereto according to thy word.
10 With my whole heart have I sought thee: O let me not wander from thy commandments.
11 Thy word have I hid in mine heart, that I might not sin against thee.
12 Blessed art thou, O LORD: teach me thy statutes.
13 With my lips have I declared all the judgments of thy mouth.
14 I have rejoiced in the way of thy testimonies, as much as in all riches.
15 I will meditate in thy precepts, and have respect unto thy ways.
16 I will delight myself in thy statutes: I will not forget thy word.
17 Deal bountifully with thy servant, that I may live, and keep thy word.

Verses begin with GIMEL ג

18 Open thou mine eyes, that I may behold wondrous things out of thy law.
19 I am a stranger in the earth: hide not thy commandments from me.
20 My soul breaketh for the longing that it hath unto thy judgments at all times.
21 Thou hast rebuked the proud that are cursed, which do err from thy commandments.
22 Remove from me reproach and contempt; for I have kept thy testimonies.
23 Princes also did sit and speak against me: but thy servant did meditate in thy statutes.
24 Thy testimonies also are my delight and my counsellors.

Verses begin with DALETH ד

... and on to the very last verse in a set of eight which begins with **TAW** ת
PSALMS 119:176 I have gone astray like a lost sheep; seek thy servant; for I do not forget thy commandments.

Each Hebrew letter has an acrostic set of eight verses. Why is this pattern of eight important when we compare it to the configuration patterns of DNA? We previously mentioned the molecules used as inter-connectors between the two spirals of DNA. At this point, rather than get into chemical formulas, we will introduce the couple of **A**ndy and **T**iffany. And then, there is a second couple with names **C**arolyn and **G**eorge. These couples are always true to each other—George is never with Tiffany nor is Andy ever with Carolyn.

Andy and Tiffany: A—T   **Carolyn and Glen: C—G**

Fig. 5.2 The A&T and the G&C DNA connectors

Now suppose that Andy and Tiffany along with Carolyn and Glen decide to go on a roller coaster ride. A roller coaster is built with room for two persons on a seat. Like DNA, a roller coaster has a structure of two rails. So, let's look at the seating configuration for the roller coaster and see how many positions that our two couples can choose.

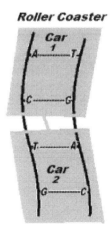

Fig. 5.3 The eight left-right positions in the roller coaster seats

How many positions are there for A&T and G&C? In car 1, A sits on the left and T sits on the right—in the meantime C sits on the left and G sits on the right. However, for car 2, we could have T on the left and A on the right—meanwhile G is on the left and C is on the right. Between the two cars, there are eight positions of A&T and G&C in relation to each other. Psalm 119 has twenty-two characters in acrostic sets of eight verses. On this page, we present a table that gives four times four times four giving sixty-four positions for the RNA (or alternately DNA) building code. We will go into much more detail about codons and the building codes in a later chapter. At this point, just note the pattern of the sixty-four slots in the table—arranged in four columns of sixteen.

RNA codon table

nonpolar | polar | basic | acidic | (stop codon)

Genetic code logo of the *Globobulimina pseudospinescens* mitochondrial genome. The logo shows the 64 codons from left to right.

Standard genetic code

1st base	2nd base				3rd base
	U	C	A	G	
U	UUU (Phe/F) Phenylalanine	UCU (Ser/S) Serine	UAU (Tyr/Y) Tyrosine	UGU (Cys/C) Cysteine	U
	UUC (Phe/F) Phenylalanine	UCC (Ser/S) Serine	UAC (Tyr/Y) Tyrosine	UGC (Cys/C) Cysteine	C
	UUA (Leu/L) Leucine	UCA (Ser/S) Serine	UAA Stop (Ochre)	UGA Stop (Opal)	A
	UUG (Leu/L) Leucine	UCG (Ser/S) Serine	UAG Stop (Amber)	UGG (Trp/W) Tryptophan	G
C	CUU (Leu/L) Leucine	CCU (Pro/P) Proline	CAU (His/H) Histidine	CGU (Arg/R) Arginine	U
	CUC (Leu/L) Leucine	CCC (Pro/P) Proline	CAC (His/H) Histidine	CGC (Arg/R) Arginine	C
	CUA (Leu/L) Leucine	CCA (Pro/P) Proline	CAA (Gln/Q) Glutamine	CGA (Arg/R) Arginine	A
	CUG (Leu/L) Leucine	CCG (Pro/P) Proline	CAG (Gln/Q) Glutamine	CGG (Arg/R) Arginine	G
A	AUU (Ile/I) Isoleucine	ACU (Thr/T) Threonine	AAU (Asn/N) Asparagine	AGU (Ser/S) Serine	U
	AUC (Ile/I) Isoleucine	ACC (Thr/T) Threonine	AAC (Asn/N) Asparagine	AGC (Ser/S) Serine	C
	AUA (Ile/I) Isoleucine	ACA (Thr/T) Threonine	AAA (Lys/K) Lysine	AGA (Arg/R) Arginine	A
	AUG[A] (Met/M) Methionine	ACG (Thr/T) Threonine	AAG (Lys/K) Lysine	AGG (Arg/R) Arginine	G
G	GUU (Val/V) Valine	GCU (Ala/A) Alanine	GAU (Asp/D) Aspartic acid	GGU (Gly/G) Glycine	U
	GUC (Val/V) Valine	GCC (Ala/A) Alanine	GAC (Asp/D) Aspartic acid	GGC (Gly/G) Glycine	C
	GUA (Val/V) Valine	GCA (Ala/A) Alanine	GAA (Glu/E) Glutamic acid	GGA (Gly/G) Glycine	A
	GUG (Val/V) Valine	GCG (Ala/A) Alanine	GAG (Glu/E) Glutamic acid	GGG (Gly/G) Glycine	G

A The codon AUG both codes for methionine and serves as an initiation site: the first AUG in an mRNA's coding region is where translation into protein begins.

Fig. 5.4 RNA codon table showing four sets of four or 64 codons total[3]
https://en.wikipedia.org/wiki/Genetic_code#RNA_codon_table (accessed 7/8/2016)

Genetically, the very hairs of our head are numbered in our inherited chromosomes—and the scriptures say as much.

LUKE 12:6 Are not five sparrows sold for two farthings, and not one of them is forgotten before God?
7 But **even the very hairs of your head are all numbered**. Fear not therefore: ye are of more value than many sparrows.

DNA has twenty-two autosomes. Are Hebrew characters the 'Lego' building blocks of DNA and for that matter the universe?

6 THE DNA AND RNA CODES

Which came first, the chicken or the egg? **DNA**—known as **D**eoxyribo**N**ucleic **A**cid and **RNA**—known as **R**ibo**N**ucleic **A**cid are quite similar in configuration and both use a twenty-two unit building code in reproduction. Think of DNA as the blueprint or template and RNA as the protein builder mechanism that makes muscles, nerves, ovaries/testes and bones, etc. that go into the human body. Since Adam was formed before he and Eve reproduced, it does appear that the human (chicken) preceded the human (egg).

Now, let's suppose you are a chef and you want to bake a protein cake. You go to the nucleus in the middle of Cell Library and you find a cookbook in which you have been told is a recipe. All you have to do is find the DNA gene recipe book, open it up and have a notepad template ready to copy down the needed ingredients.

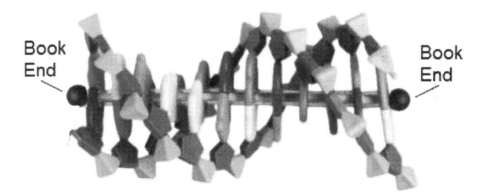

Fig. 6.1 The DNA spiral with the A-T and G-C connectors.

Now you run into a bit of problem—you have to lift one of the spirals apart from the other so you can copy down the recipe more efficiently on to your note pad. No problem, the DNA strand seems to 'know' that you want to copy the recipe and it opens up. The DNA recipe configuration is G—C, G—C, C—G, C—G, T—A, A—T, G—C and A—T. So, you copy down the ingredients on each line of your notebook—that was easy. In fact, it was too easy, because you soon learn that the ingredient "T" has been banned by the Proteinland government. You will have to find a substitute and the footnote says to use the ingredient "U" as a substitute. What is this elusive "U". We will find that A has changed into a U.

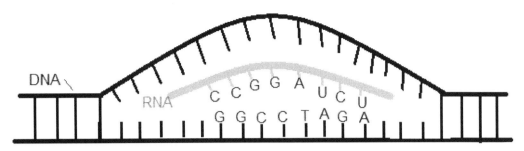

Fig. 6.2 A DNA spiral opens up so that its formula can be copied to an RNA template.

Once the RNA strand receives its coding, it departs from the DNA strand and the DNA strand closes. Then, the RNA strand goes on to be the blueprint of building blocks for a protein. But this is a protein and a protein can't use a **T**—it must build with a **U**.

We have said that **A**ndy and **T**iffany are a happy couple and are always seen together. However, doubts have arisen because when **A**ndy goes to Proteinland, he has a girl friend named **U**rsula. Is this a lover's triangle or what?

In order to avoid having the trees block our view of the overall forest, we have used the codes of A—T and G—C and now we have introduced U. It is now time to look at the chemical biography of the A, T, G, C and U group. We will fist check out **G**len and **C**arolyn.

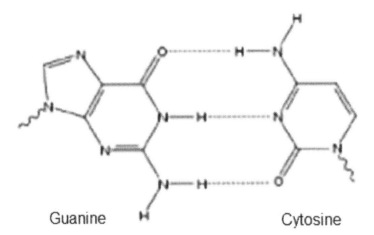

Fig. 6.3 The triple hydrogen bonds between Guanine and Cytosine

Glen and Carolyn are like two lovers that not only hold both hands together, but also are always kissing each other—a total of three bonds attracting them together.

Next, we will visit Andy and Tiffany. They don't like to be seen kissing in public, but they are constantly holding hands.

Andy Adenine & *Tiffany Thymine*

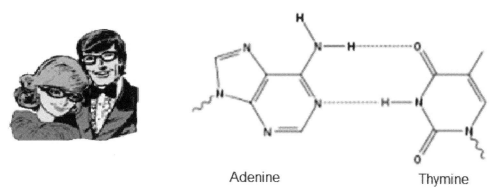

Fig. 6.4 The double hydrogen bond between Adenine and Thymine

Now, why is it that when Andy is in DNA land, he is always seen with Tiffany. But, when he goes into RNA land, he has a new companion, her name is Ursula. Well, like Superman and his famous metamorphism in the phone booth, Tiffany has a secret, she transforms into Ursula Uracil when she enters the phone booth and then travels to Proteinland. All she has to do in the phone booth is tuck in her hair a bit and she changes from thymine to uracil.

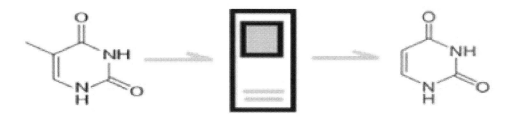

Fig. 6.5 The change-over from Thymine to Uracil

If we were to have nano or better vision to see within the human cell, it might appear to us like a busy city. It has manufacturing plants, trains supplying raw materials, quality control inspectors and vehicles traveling all over the place. How does all this traffic 'know' what routes to take and how do the various parts know how to come together. In the next chapter, we will meet a lady name CoDonna who is a traffic supervisor and we will use the twenty-two unit RNA code to actually build a protein.

In chapter 3 of this book, we referenced this scripture about the rods (or spindles) that are involved in the mitosis or division of cells.

EZEKIEL 19:10 Thy mother is like a **vine in thy blood**, planted by the waters: **she was fruitful and full of branches by reason of many waters**.
11 And she had **strong rods for the sceptres of them that bare rule**, and her stature was exalted among the thick branches, and she appeared in her height with the multitude of her branches.

Below is a depiction of a cell going through mitosis (division into two cells). The rods can be seen like the reinforcing spokes of an umbrella on each side of the cell. Information is being transmitted through these rods or microtubules as they are called. When all is complete, the cell divides.

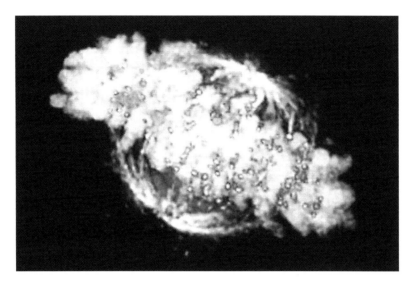

Fig. 6.6 A fluorescence micrograph of a cell during metaphase of mitosis.
Credit: DR PAUL ANDREWS, UNIVERSITY OF DUNDEE/Science Photo Library/Getty Images[4]
http://biology.about.com/od/mitosisglossary/g/spindle_fibers.htm

GENESIS 30:38   And he set **the rods which he had pilled before the flocks in the gutters in the watering troughs** when the flocks came to drink, that they should conceive when they came to drink.

For those who want to dig deeper into this subject, consider the **phrase *vine in thy blood, planted by the waters*** from Ezekiel 19:10, Jacob setting ***the rods in the gutters before the water troughs*** and also the Spirit of God hovering over ***the waters*** in Genesis 1:2. The function of microtubules and the **quantum coherent state of ordered water** (rather than a **chaotic** state of water) transmitting signals through the microtubule is discussed on pages 357 to 369 of Roger Penrose's book ***Shadows of the Mind***.

The concept of an ordered, cohesive signal transmission medium is something that scientists have had some success at achieving at temperatures just above absolute zero (-273 Celsius, or - 460 Fahrenheit). The idea that "ordered" water could exist at human body temperatures in the microtubules of the human brain is extremely intriguing—particularly since water in its "normal" state is chaotic.

Genesis 1:2 And **the earth was without order**, and empty; and darkness was upon the face of the deep. And the Spirit of God moved upon the **face of the waters**.   Jubilee Bible 2000

7 THE TWENTY-TWO LETTER PROTEIN BUILDING CODE

Now that we have identified the basic characters (or building blocks) in the DNA and RNA codes, our next step will be to become acquainted with CoDonna, the traffic director, who gives instructions for assembling the building blocks.

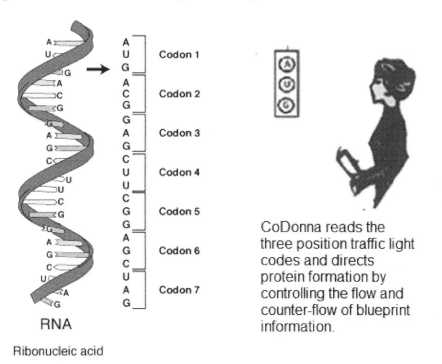

Fig. 7.1 RNA assembly diagram and representation of a three position codon reader.[5]
https://upload.wikimedia.org/wikipedia/commons/d/d4/RNA-codons.png (accessed 7/4/2016 Illustration by TransControl on Creative Commons)

Both the DNA building code and the RNA building code are based on three letter codons. Codons can be likened to a stop-light which has the **three** positions of red, yellow and green. See the table below which has the three letter codes for building DNA.

Inverse table (compressed using IUPAC notation)

#	Amino acid	Codons	#	Amino acid	Codons
1	Ala/A	GCT, GCC, GCA, GCG	12	Leu/L	TTA, TTG, CTT, CTC, CTA, CTG
2	Arg/R	CGT, CGC, CGA, CGG, AGA, AGG	13	Lys/K	AAA, AAG
3	Asn/N	AAT, AAC	14	Met/M	ATG
4	Asp/D	GAT, GAC	15	Phe/F	TTT, TTC
5	Cys/C	TGT, TGC	16	Pro/P	CCT, CCC, CCA, CCG
6	Gln/Q	CAA, CAG	17	Ser/S	TCT, TCC, TCA, TCG, AGT, AGC
7	Glu/E	GAA, GAG	18	Thr/T	ACT, ACC, ACA, ACG
8	Gly/G	GGT, GGC, GGA, GGG	19	Trp/W	TGG
9	His/H	CAT, CAC	20	Tyr/Y	TAT, TAC
10	Ile/I	ATT, ATC, ATA	21	Val/V	GTT, GTC, GTA, GTG
11	START	ATG	22	STOP	TAA, TGA, TAG

Fig. 7.2 DNA Building Table Excerpt[6]

It is quite remarkable that the START position is in the #11 slot and its code is ATG. And the STOP position is in the # 22 slot and it can have three codes which can end the building process. Number 11 is a half-multiple of 22 and of course number 22 matches the Hebrew alphabet.

Now here is something else remarkable. If we want to build a **RNA protein**, we must place the letter **U** in place of the letter **T**. **The same exact positions in the building table work for both DNA and RNA.** START becomes AUG and STOP can be UAA, UGA or UAG.

We will now call upon **CoDonna** the traffic director to help us make a RNA **protein**. And to start the process, she will read the #11 slot **START** code as **AUG** to begin to assemble a protein. Note in the following table, the code Asp/D exists in the #4 slot. This is an amino acid that is used as a building block for more complex proteins and is assembled by using the three position codons GAU and GAC. Amino acids are often used to form protein chains because they are acid on one end of the molecule and basic on the other end. They hook together in chains like cars on a train.

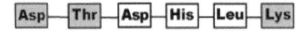

Fig. 7.3 A protein built by using the RNA code

Let's build a protein. We START our process at the #11 slot with AUG. Then, we need to build **Asp** with GAU, GAC from the #4 slot. Next is **Thr** from the #18 slot using ACU, ACC, ACA, ACG and then to **Asp** once again using GAU and GAC. Using the above table, we will continue to work our way through **His** and **Leu** until we come to **Lys** which is coded in the #13 slot and utilizes AAA and AAG. And since we have now reached the end of our protein, we need to STOP the process, so we would use one of the codes in slot #22, for our example we will use UAA. We have just built a protein!

We will pose a little story about CoDonna's work in building proteins. It seems that Andy and Tiffany/Ursula, Glen and Carolyn all have mirror image twins. These twins, being a mirror image, are all found to be right handed. In the meantime, Andy, Tiffany, Glen and Carolyn/Ursula are all left handed. The mirror image twins wanted to be part of the protein building process, but CoDonna had some bad news for them—she could only use left-handers in the protein building process. The mirror image twins asked why and CoDonna replied, "You will have ask God. All I know is that **all** DNA and **all** proteins **require left handed** amino acids."

This little story hearkens back to the Harold Urey-Stanley Miller experiments of the 1950's. They mixed together compounds in a flask which were thought to be present in the earth's early atmosphere and introduced electrical arcing within the flask. Sure enough some of the amino acids that have been identified in the protein building process were formed. There was one problem, the compounds formed were a mixture of right handed (dextro) molecules and left handed (levo) molecules. While dextro and levo compounds appear to be the same, they may have different boiling points and do rotate light in opposite directions. (We have already discussed the microtubules as being wave guides. Wave guides must have a consistent rotation to truly transmit signals and avoid babble). There was no 'molecule picker' within the Urey-Miller flask to separate the dextro compounds from the levo compounds.

But, let's suppose there was a molecule picker that separated out all the levo compounds and they were linked up like rail ties in perfect order on a DNA track. Scientists have been able to gene splice and have been able to make clones—but **they have had to start with a seed of life that was already present.** What is the source of that spark of life that could enliven the lifeless synthetic railroad track DNA structures?

GENESIS 1:3 And God said, Let there be light: and **there was light**.

JOHN 1:9 That was the true Light, **which lighteth every man that cometh into the world**.

8 CHROMOSOMES AND GENES

10,000,000,000,000 Plus and Counting …

Scientist's estimates on the **total number of cells** in the human body vary considerably, but rest assured it is a huge number. The diagram below depicts just one of these human cells. Each cell has a nucleus and within the cell are twenty-two autosomes from the mother and twenty-two autosomes from the father. And then within the chromosomes are genes. The number of genes at this point is estimated somewhere in the 20,000 plus range for a set of twenty-three chromosomes.

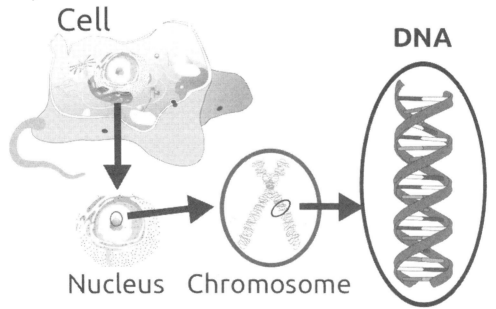

Fig. 8.1 Overview of cell, its nucleus, a chromosome and the DNA spiral ladder
https://en.wikipedia.org/wiki/Chromosome#/media/File:Eukaryote_DNA-en.svg (accessed 7/4/2016)[7]

Now, here is an amazing fact. **Each** one of the 10,000,000,000,000 plus cells has a nucleus with chromosomes within it. This nucleus **within each cell** contains the chromosome blueprints for **all** the human body parts. In the next minute your body will have made about 30,000 skin cells to replace shed cells. Think of having ten trillion plus public libraries residing with your body. Who could have programmed/engineered such an amazing feat?

Mankind's 'discovery' of DNA was credited to Francis Crick and James Watson of King's College in 1953. However, the project to map essentially one human genome was formally launched in 1990 and completed in 2003—a thirteen year effort. And yet, DNA 'knows' how to replicate itself dating back from antiquity.

Next we will look at the estimated number of genes for chromosomes 1 through 23. These are shown in the partial table and graphics below.

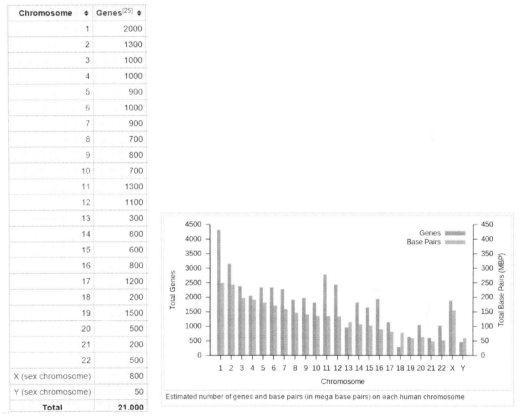

Chromosome	Genes[25]
1	2000
2	1300
3	1000
4	1000
5	900
6	1000
7	900
8	700
9	800
10	700
11	1300
12	1100
13	300
14	800
15	600
16	800
17	1200
18	200
19	1500
20	500
21	200
22	500
X (sex chromosome)	800
Y (sex chromosome)	50
Total	21,000

Fig. 8.2 Tabulation of base pairs of genes for autosomes and X or Y chromosomes
https://en.wikipedia.org/wiki/Chromosome; (accessed 6/24/2016) Partial table from Sanger Institute's human genome information in the Vertebrate Genome Annotation (VEGA) database[8]

Chromosome 1 has the most gene pairs—about 2000. The total number adds up to about 21,000. In the interest of correlation with the twenty-two letters of the Hebrew alphabet and the twenty-two autosomes, we thought that the gene total might add up to 22,000. But, these numbers are estimated and we won't try to nudge them toward a correlation number we like—let the chips fall where they may.

Now, since we have been comparing the Hebrew alphabet and its acrostics to the twenty-two autosomes, it is worthwhile to look at the Hebrew alphabet numbering system. Frankly, we find it odd. The first ten characters are numbered one to ten. But beyond that, it jumps by ten for each character. And when it reaches 100, it jumps by 100 for each character until the number of 400 is reached for Taw, the 22nd character. Obviously, there is some methodology to this—but we are not sure what it is. We now present the Hebrew character numbering table and will look at it in more detail later in this chapter.

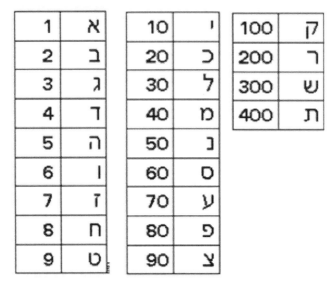

Fig. 8.3 Hebrew character numbering system (1 to 400)

So far, we have primarily focused on the Psalm 119 acrostic because it seems to be the master key for the Hebrew language. But, as we shall find out in the next chapter, there are many acrostics in the Psalms, also in Proverbs 31 and Lamentations. Lamentations has a very unusual pattern in that the first four chapters are acrostic and the fifth chapter, while not acrostic, has a 22 verse pattern.

As one might surmise by its name, Lamentations is not a book that you would recommend to your friends to cheer them up. Could there be hidden in its acrostics, coding for some of mankind's woes?

EXODUS 15:26 And said, If thou wilt diligently hearken to the voice of the LORD thy God, and wilt do that which is right in his sight, and wilt give ear to his commandments, and keep all his statutes, **I will put none of these diseases upon thee, which I have brought upon the Egyptians**: for I am the LORD that healeth thee.

Scientists have made considerable advances in identifying mutations or defects in the DNA which are causative of certain diseases. Further, they have identified in which chromosome the defect occurs. Here is list of defects (accessed 6/25/2016 from Human Genome Project) as listed in Wikipedia for chromosome one:

Bible Acrostic Code Mysteries

"There are 890 known diseases related to this chromosome. Some of these diseases are hearing loss, Alzheimer disease, glaucoma and breast cancer. Rearrangements and mutations of chromosome 1 are prevalent in cancer and many other diseases. Patterns of sequence variation reveal signals of recent selection in specific genes that may contribute to human fitness, and also in regions where no function is evident. The following diseases are some of those related to genes on chromosome 1 (which contains the most known genetic diseases of any human chromosome). See this website for list of diseases for the chromosomes. https://en.wikipedia.org/wiki/Chromosome_1_(human)#Diseases_and_disorders[9]

1q21.1 deletion syndrome
1q21.1 duplication syndrome
Alzheimer disease
Alzheimer disease, type 4
Breast cancer
Brooke Greenberg Disease (Syndrome X)
Carnitine palmitoyltransferase II deficiency
Charcot–Marie–Tooth disease, types 1 and 2
collagenopathy, types II and XI
congenital hypothyroidism
Ehlers-Danlos syndrome
Ehlers-Danlos syndrome, kyphoscoliosis type
Factor V Leiden thrombophilia
Familial adenomatous polyposis
galactosemia
Gaucher disease
Gaucher disease type 1
Gaucher disease type 2
Gaucher disease type 3
Gaucher-like disease
Gelatinous drop-like corneal dystrophy
Glaucoma
Hearing loss, autosomal recessive deafness 36
Hemochromatosis
Hemochromatosis, type 2
Hepatoerythropoietic porphyria
Homocystinuria
Hutchinson Gilford Progeria Syndrome
3-hydroxy-3-methylglutaryl-CoA lyase deficiency
Hypertrophic cardiomyopathy, autosomal dominant mutations of TNNT2; hypertrophy usually mild; restrictive phenotype may be present; may carry high risk of sudden cardiac death
maple syrup urine disease
medium-chain acyl-coenzyme A dehydrogenase deficiency
Microcephaly
Muckle-Wells Syndrome
Nonsyndromic deafness
Nonsyndromic deafness, autosomal dominant
Nonsyndromic deafness, autosomal recessive
Oligodendroglioma
Parkinson disease
Pheochromocytoma
porphyria
porphyria cutanea tarda

popliteal pterygium syndrome
prostate cancer
Stickler syndrome
Stickler syndrome, COL11A1
TAR syndrome
trimethylaminuria
Usher syndrome
Usher syndrome type II
Van der Woude syndrome
Variegate porphyria
https://en.wikipedia.org/wiki/Chromosome_1_(human)#Diseases_and_disorders

Before we leave this chapter, we want to revisit the Hebrew character numbering system and present for our readers some preliminary explorations. A simple line plot of the value of the character's associated number versus the twenty-two characters looks like this.

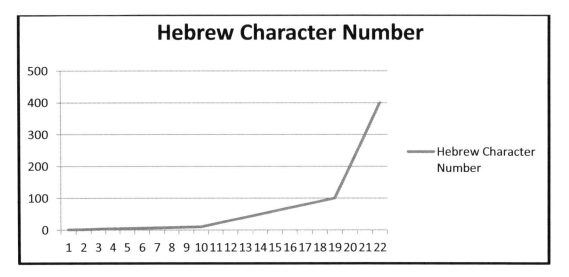

Fig. 8.4 Plot of Hebrew character number versus the number of Hebrew characters

The data curve looks exponential so we will explore it a bit further by calculating the natural logarithm (Ln) of each number. Like π, the natural logarithm system is derived from a base commonly called "e" which is an unending number. It is usually rounded off to a value of 2.72.

Why does π have a value of 3.14… and e have a value of 2.72…? A good question.

Since this series may not end with the 22nd character Taw with a value, we will extend the series to a 44th character. The series from 1 to 10 is like our normal numbering system. And then we come to the eleven node. Instead of an expected eleven, it jumps to 20, 30, 40, 50, 60, 70, 80, 90, and 100. Then, it jumps to 200, 300 and then the twenty-second node is 400. So maybe this numbering system doesn't just stop at 400.

So, using the series rationale, we would add 500, 600, 700, 800, 900, 1000, 2000, 3000, 4000, 5000 until we reach the third multiple of eleven or the thirty-third node. After

that, we continue to the forty-four node: 6000, 7000, 8000, 9000, 10000, 20000, 30000, 40000, 50000, 60000, 70000, 80000 …

It has been said that the Hebrew Language is cyclic and has cycles within cycles—what patterns will we find?

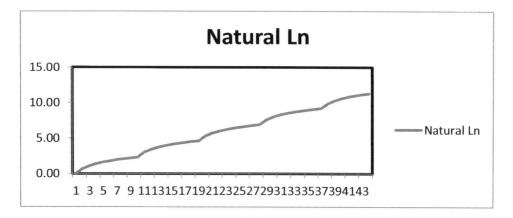

Fig. 8.5 Plot of natural logarithm of Hebrew character number versus 44 characters

Inspection of the data shows the presence of cycles as if something is increasing in a spiral. If you flashback to chapter 4, you will remember the cycles of eleven that we associated with the total seen and unseen universe dimensions. And then, from Chapter 7 we saw that the protein (and also the DNA) building table (IUPAC notation) had STARTS and STOPS at the eleven node and the twenty-second node.

11 - START: AUG   22 - STOP: UAA, UGA, UAG

Added to the above co-incidences, we see the 'escape velocity' for a daughter fractal to escape from its mother—and how that is related to eleven cycles culminating in a multiple of π. (see chapter 4). When one looks at how the numbers spiraling on the graph which are tamed into nice looking little rainbow lines, one wonders where the very first fractal got started.

1KINGS 4:33 And he spake of trees, **from the cedar tree** that is in Lebanon even unto the hyssop that springeth out of the wall: he spake also of beasts, and of fowl, and of creeping things, and of fishes.
34 And there came of all people to hear the wisdom of Solomon, from all kings of the earth, which had heard of his wisdom.

Was there an Adam cedar tree fractal and an Eve cedar tree fractal that initially began the numerous as the sands of sea male and female cedar trees that exist on this planet today? Who knoweth how many replications of fractals have occurred since the beginning?

Fig. 8.6 From PBS website program aired August 24, 2011: "*Hunting the Hidden Dimension*; Mysteriously beautiful fractals are shaking up the world of mathematics and deepening our understanding of nature." [http://www.pbs.org/wgbh/nova/physics/hunting-hidden-dimension.html accessed 7/4/2016][10]

So, let's take a look at the values for e and also for π and inspect them for cycles of multiples of eleven.

3.14159265358979323846264**33**83279502**88**41971693**99**375105820974**44**592307816406286208**99**86280348253421**11**7067982148086513282306**66**470938**44**609**55**058**22**317253594081284811**11**745028410270193852**11055**596**44**6229489549303819**644**28109756**65**9**33**4**4**6128475648**233**7867831652712019091456485**66**9234603486104543266482133936072602491412737245870**06** ...

2.71828182845904523536028747135266249775724709369995957496696276630353547594571382178525166427427466391932003059921817413596629043572900334295260595630738132328627943490763233829880753195251019011573834187930702154089149934884167509244761460668082264800168477411853742345442437107539077744992069 ...

You can see and compare the multiples of eleven that are present in both π and e. It does appear that a relationship exists in our natural, every day world. However, is this just random generation of twin numbers—or is it something much more profound?

Mathematicians have an imaginary world and in this world often use the symbol *i*. Mathematically *i* is defined as the **square root of minus one**. Electrical and electronic engineers poke their hands into this 'imaginary' world, do all kinds of calculations and then

square the square root of minus one—which is one—to get their valuable results back into what we call the 'real' world. **e** and π may have a flirtatious relationship in our 'seen' world, but, as we shall soon see, are lovers in the 'unseen' world.

Our physics friends have discussed how the total of seen and unseen dimensions were resolved by string theory's super-symmetry. Complicated considerations were resolved by an over-arching principle. The New Testament speaks of ***the simplicity that is in Christ.*** Is it possible that these two equations have profound implications in the configuration of the universe?

For fractals: $Z_{n+1} = [Z_n]^2 + C$

For the relationship between e and π. $e^{\pi i} + 1 = 0$

Hopefully our math, physics and biology friends can help in answering this question.

9 ACROSTICS IN PROVERBS, PSALMS AND LAMENTATIONS

When one mentions Bible acrostics, the thoughts almost always turn to Psalm 119. But, digging a little deeper, we find acrostics in many places in the scriptures—and given our exploratory inclinations into the scientific area, we wonder what nuggets and gems of information may be hidden in their content. Will the diseases resulting from defects in the human DNA be repaired such that we may walk in a land that *the vulture's eye hath not seen*? What *thing that is hid* will be brought *to light*?

JOB 28:1 Surely there is a vein for the silver, and a place for gold where they fine it. …
6 The stones of it are the place of sapphires: and it hath dust of gold.
7 **There is a path which no fowl knoweth,** and **which the vulture's eye hath not seen**: …
9 He putteth forth his hand upon the rock; **he overturneth the mountains by the roots**.
10 He cutteth out rivers among the rocks; and his eye seeth every precious thing.
11 He bindeth the floods from overflowing; and **the thing that is hid bringeth he forth to light**.

As we begin to examine the various acrostics, we will find some where a letter is missing. This is particularly true in the Psalms (other than Psalm 119). Like in DNA, it is difficult to know if something was mutated from the original, or if copies of copies of copies resulted in something being left out. In some cases, the character that is missing in the KJV related translations can be found in versions such as the Syriac. However, some think that a character may have been purposely left out in the series to make a point.

Let's start with an acrostic from Proverbs chapter 31. You may recognize it from what is commonly known as the virtuous woman passages, but may not have realized that it was an acrostic. The Hebrew sentences read from right to left and the English translation reads from left to right. Translation from Hebrew to English does not always result in the first word in the English sentence matching up with the first word in a Hebrew sentence. Therefore, the **English word** which corresponds to the **first Hebrew word** has been **bolded**. Also, the numbers corresponding to each Hebrew character are displayed.

So, take some time and take in the wisdom and the structure of the excellent wife in the Proverbs chapter 31 acrostic in the following array.

See **http://www.mechon-mamre.org/p/pt/pt2831.htm** (accessed 6/29/2016) for basic Proverb's 31 text before enhancements were made for this chapter's presentation.

Proverbs Chapter 31 מִשְׁלֵי

אֵשֶׁת-חַיִל, מִי יִמְצָא; וְרָחֹק מִפְּנִינִים מִכְרָהּ.	**10** A **woman** of valour who can find? for her price is far above rubies. ----------ALEPH [1]
בָּטַח בָּהּ, לֵב בַּעְלָהּ; וְשָׁלָל, לֹא יֶחְסָר.	**11** The heart of her husband doth safely **trust** in her, and he hath no lack of gain. - BETH[2]
גְּמָלַתְהוּ טוֹב וְלֹא-רָע-- כֹּל, יְמֵי חַיֶּיהָ.	**12** She **doeth** him good and not evil all the days of her life. -----------------------GIMEL [3]
דָּרְשָׁה, צֶמֶר וּפִשְׁתִּים; וַתַּעַשׂ, בְּחֵפֶץ כַּפֶּיהָ.	**13** She **seeketh** wool and flax, and worketh willingly with her hands. ---------DALETH [4]
הָיְתָה, כָּאֳנִיּוֹת סוֹחֵר; מִמֶּרְחָק, תָּבִיא לַחְמָהּ.	**14** **She** is like the merchant-ships; she bringeth her food from afar. ---------- HEY [5]
וַתָּקָם, בְּעוֹד לַיְלָה--וַתִּתֵּן טֶרֶף לְבֵיתָהּ; וְחֹק, לְנַעֲרֹתֶיהָ.	**15** She riseth **also** while it is yet night, and giveth food to her household, and a portion to her maidens. -------------------------WAW [6]
זָמְמָה שָׂדֶה, וַתִּקָּחֵהוּ; מִפְּרִי כַפֶּיהָ, נטע (נָטְעָה) כָּרֶם.	**16** She **considereth** a field, and buyeth it; with the fruit of her hands she planteth a vineyard. -------------------------------ZAYIN [7]
חָגְרָה בְעוֹז מָתְנֶיהָ; וַתְּאַמֵּץ, זְרוֹעֹתֶיהָ.	**17** She **girdeth** her loins with strength, and maketh strong her arms. -------------HETH [8]
טָעֲמָה, כִּי-טוֹב סַחְרָהּ; לֹא-יִכְבֶּה בליל (בַלַּיְלָה) נֵרָהּ.	**18** She **perceiveth** that her merchandise is good; her lamp goeth not out by night. -- TETH [9]
יָדֶיהָ, שִׁלְּחָה בַכִּישׁוֹר; וְכַפֶּיהָ, תָּמְכוּ פָלֶךְ.	**19** She layeth her **hands** to the distaff, and her hands hold the spindle. -------------- YOD [10]
כַּפָּהּ, פָּרְשָׂה לֶעָנִי; וְיָדֶיהָ, שִׁלְּחָה לָאֶבְיוֹן.	**20** She stretcheth out her **hand** to the poor; yea, she reacheth forth her hands to the needy. ------------------------------- KAPH [20]
לֹא-תִירָא לְבֵיתָהּ מִשָּׁלֶג: כִּי כָל-בֵּיתָהּ, לָבֻשׁ שָׁנִים.	**21** She is **not** afraid of the snow for her household; for all her household are clothed with scarlet. ---------------------- LAMED [30]

מַרְבַדִּים עָשְׂתָה-לָּהּ; שֵׁשׁ וְאַרְגָּמָן לְבוּשָׁהּ.	**22** She maketh for herself **coverlets**; her clothing is fine linen and purple. — MEM [40]
נוֹדָע בַּשְּׁעָרִים בַּעְלָהּ; בְּשִׁבְתּוֹ, עִם-זִקְנֵי-אָרֶץ.	**23** Her husband is **known** in the gates, when he sitteth among the elders of the land. -- NUN [50]
סָדִין עָשְׂתָה, וַתִּמְכֹּר; וַחֲגוֹר, נָתְנָה לַכְּנַעֲנִי.	**24** She maketh **linen** garments and selleth them; and delivereth girdles unto the merchant. -------------------------------- SAMEK [60]
עֹז-וְהָדָר לְבוּשָׁהּ; וַתִּשְׂחַק, לְיוֹם אַחֲרוֹן.	**25 Strength** and dignity are her clothing; and she laugheth at the time to come. –AYIN [70]
פִּיהָ, פָּתְחָה בְחָכְמָה; וְתוֹרַת חֶסֶד, עַל-לְשׁוֹנָהּ.	**26** She openeth her **mouth** with wisdom; and the law of kindness is on her tongue. -- PEY [80]
צוֹפִיָּה, הילכות (הֲלִיכוֹת) בֵּיתָהּ; וְלֶחֶם עַצְלוּת, לֹא תֹאכֵל.	**27** She **looketh** well to the ways of her household, and eateth not the bread of idleness. ---------------------------- TSADE [90]
קָמוּ בָנֶיהָ, וַיְאַשְּׁרוּהָ; בַּעְלָהּ, וַיְהַלְלָהּ.	**28** Her children **rise up**, and call her blessed; her husband also, and he praiseth her: -- KOPH [100]
רַבּוֹת בָּנוֹת, עָשׂוּ חָיִל; וְאַתְּ, עָלִית עַל-כֻּלָּנָה.	**29** 'Many daughters have done valiantly, but thou excellest them all.' ----------- RESH [200]
שֶׁקֶר הַחֵן, וְהֶבֶל הַיֹּפִי: אִשָּׁה יִרְאַת-יְהוָה, הִיא תִתְהַלָּל.	**30** Grace is **deceitful**, and beauty is vain; but a woman that feareth the LORD, she shall be praised. ------------------------------- SHIN [300]
תְּנוּ-לָהּ, מִפְּרִי יָדֶיהָ; וִיהַלְלוּהָ בַשְּׁעָרִים מַעֲשֶׂיהָ. {ש}	**31 Give** her of the fruit of her hands; and let her works praise her in the gates. -- TAW [400]

Now that we have looked at a complete acrostic in Proverbs and considered its structure, its characters, its numbers and its parallels with the English language, we will devote some time to considering what some other Bible teachers over the years have said about acrostics.

In general, most of the commentaries have described acrostics as having poetic beauty and providing strong indication that what is written is the A to Z of the thought. Or, perhaps we should say the Hebrew Aleph to Taw or in Greek, the Alpha and Omega. Some have offered that acrostics provide a mnemonic memory aid for a sequence of scriptures or themes. Other than literary excellence, there have been few suggestions that the acrostics contained a code. Some commentaries even fail to mention that the subject scriptures even exist as an acrostic. However, we will look at some of the references that describe them in more detail.

Bible Acrostic Code Mysteries

We will begin with information from the Bible Researcher website[11] (http://www.bible-researcher.com/acrostics.html accessed 6/27/2016). This website gives valuable background information about acrostics. It provides this quote from J.A. Motyer:

> "J.A. Motyer describes this feature as "a poetic way of saying that a total coverage of the subject was being offered."
>
> In the common form of acrostic found in Old Testament Poetry, each line or stanza begins with a letter of the Hebrew alphabet in order. This literary form may have been intended as an aid to memory, but more likely it was a poetic way of saying that a total coverage of the subject was being offered -- as we would say, 'from A to Z.' Acrostics occur in Psalms 111 and 112, where each letter begins a line; in Psalms 25, 34, and 145, where each letter begins a half-verse; in Psalm 37, Proverbs 31:10-31, and Lamentations 1, 2, and 4, where each letter begins a whole verse; and in Lamentations 3, where each letter begins three verses. Psalm 119 is the most elaborate demonstration of the acrostic method where, in each section of eight verses, the same opening letter is used, and the twenty-two sections of the psalm move through the Hebrew alphabet, letter after letter. --J.A. Motyer, "Acrostic," in *The New International Dictionary of the Bible* (Grand Rapids: Zondervan, 1987), p. 12." *******

We has just reviewed the acrostics in Psalm 119 and Proverbs 31—but here is a whole new list of acrostics: Psalms 25, 34, 37, 112, 113 and 145. And add to that, the rather complete sets of acrostics in Lamentations chapters 1 through 4. What gems will we find in all these scriptures?

Another commentary which gives abundant information is from an abstract: Hebrew Alphabetic Acrostics – Significance and Translation; ROELIE VAN DER SPUY[12]; NORTH WEST UNIVERSITY, SOUTH AFRICA AND SIL INTERNATIONAL; *ABSTRACT*: Van der Spuy: Hebrew Alphabetic Acrostics *OTE* 21/2 (2008), 513-532 513 An excerpt is as follows:

> "When thinking of acrostic passages, the Psalms mostly come to mind, but there are also many other passages that form part of the Hebrew alphabetic acrostic literature. Ps 119 is one of the most complete and extensive examples of a Hebrew alphabetic acrostic psalm. For many this is the only known alphabetic acrostic in the Bible.
>
> Here is a list of all acrostic passages in the Hebrew Bible:
> Psalm 9-10 Each Hebrew consonant covers two verses. These two psalms form one acrostic unit. Because of text-critical problems and the fact that they are presented as two separate Psalms, they are not always included in the list of acrostics. In the Septuagint they constitute one psalm (http://bible1.wordpress.com/tag/psalms/ Accessed 16 March 2007).

Psalm 25 Each Hebrew consonant covers 1 verse.
Psalm 34 Each Hebrew consonant covers 1 verse.
Psalm 37 Each Hebrew consonant covers 2 verses.
Psalm 111 Each Hebrew consonant covers ½ verse.
Psalm 112 Each Hebrew consonant covers ½ verse.
Psalm 119 Each Hebrew consonant covers 8 verses.
Psalm 145 Each Hebrew consonant covers 1 verse.

Lam 1- 4 In chapter 1 and 2 each Hebrew consonant covers 1 verse which consists of 3 stanzas. In chapter 3 each consonant covers 3 stanzas/verses, therefore it has 66 verses. Chapter 4 has 22 verses, each consonant consists of 2 stanzas beginning with that letter of the alphabet. Chapter 5 has 22 verses, but is not an alphabetic acrostic.

Prov 31: 10 –31 Each Hebrew consonant covers 1 verse.
Nahum 1: 1- 9 The Aleph covers three lines. There seems to be an interjection of 2 lines before the rest of the consonants, which covers only one verse each. The letter zayin appears in the second position of the line."

****

Another great source of information about acrostics is from appendices 60 and 63 of *The Companion Bible* which has compiled the prodigious works of E.W. Bullinger. The plethora of information contained in the appendices alone is worth the purchase of this Bible. As we further examine the information in the various Psalms and other books, we will reference some of the comments from these appendices. Bullinger also provides us with some leads about acrostics in the book of Esther—a book hitherto not mentioned.

So, the question arises now that we have presented all this background information about acrostics. Why are we doing this and where is it leading? What are our goals?—we will cover that in the next two chapters.

10 THE ROOTS OF HEBREW LANGUAGE

Now, that we have used the Proverbs 31 text to introduce the general form and structure of an acrostic, it is time to look at language itself. There are obvious questions to consider—why is the original Hebrew devoid of vowels? And why does the first Hebrew word in the acrostic not consistently match the first word in the English translation? What were the actual characters used in the very original Hebrew?—for instance what characters were used to write the ten commandments?

There are quite controversial viewpoints on the beginnings of language. There is the secular viewpoint and there is viewpoint held by the Rabbi's. Unfortunately, the Rabbis have their own multiple interpretations about which is the proper, original Hebrew alphabet. The Dead Sea scrolls did provide additional confirmations about the early alphabet, but still, it is difficult to say this version or that version is the true, pure original Hebrew language. So, it is not our purpose here to say the text that we have selected (the Mechon-Mamre text) to illustrate acrostics is the "one". It is simply the text we have chosen to illustrate acrostics because it gives a good "split screen" display of comparative English and ancient Hebrew text. See their website: http://www.mechon-mamre.org/p/pt/pt0.htm . There are many other sources available such as Bible Hub http://biblehub.com/ and the JPS (Jewish Publication Society) website https://jps.org/ .

We will begin by looking at language as viewed from a secular viewpoint. Studies of language initially assumed a gradual transition from Egyptian hieroglyphics to an alphabet. But, more recent information suggests a more abrupt transition to the alphabet which resulted from a Semitic source. David Sacks, in his book, **Letter Perfect,** discusses the beginning of the alphabet. On page 17 of his book, Sachs outlines the conclusions of Yale Egyptology professor, John Darnell who investigated myriad carvings at Wadi-el-Hol which is about 30 miles northwest of Luxor, Egypt.

> "By 1998, Darnell and others had reached a couple of dramatic conclusions. First, the two inscriptions are probably the oldest alphabetic writing yet discovered, certainly the oldest that can be dated confidently: They were carved in in about

1800 B.C., give or take a century. More important, the inscriptions can be viewed as signposts that point directly back to the alphabet's invention. On the basis of the Wadi-el-Hol evidence, that invention is now assigned to around 2000 B.C. in Egypt—about three centuries earlier (and in a different country) than previously thought. "Finds in Egypt Date Alphabet in Earlier Era," announced the front-page *New York Times* headline of a November 1999 piece reporting on the work. …
Who were the inventors? Darnell believes they may have been in the Egyptian army: Semitic mercenaries or similar, whom the Egyptians would have called *Amu* (Asiatics). …
One last item of information. Quite near to one of the alphabetic inscriptions on the limestone wall is an Egyptian message mentioning someone named Bebi, titled as "expedition leader of the *Amu*." This can't be co-incidence, Darnell maintains: The three inscriptions, alphabetic and Egyptian, were probably carved at the same time. If Bebi was Egyptian, leading a Semite troop on road patrol, then the "chief" of one alphabetic message could have been one of those Semites, a junior officer or tribal chieftain under Bebi's command." *******

Where did our alphabet come from and who is this Bebi? We wish we knew who Bebi was. Moses started out as an Egyptian official. And then we do have a particular scripture which indicates a source of alphabetical writing. Moses records the event: *And the LORD delivered unto me two tables of stone written with the finger of God*. The first five books of the Bible are generally ascribed to Moses' authorship.

A typical journey with Ancient Hebrew Roots is a journey by stages—a struggle with the Hebrew code begins with Bible translations. Many of them only give a small hint to the ancient Hebrew root. Then comes reading multiple books that share Hebrew word studies. Studying modern Hebrew lexicons without seeing the verbal Hebrew ancient root is like trying to unscramble eggs.

We will start with the Paleo-Hebrew alphabet which is corroborated by archeological evidence showing more common use of the script in about the 10th century BC. However when the Jews were taken into Babylonian captivity, the original Hebrew began to morph into the Aramaic with the addition of vowels and this became the Hebrew writing of Jesus' time. Eventually, the 'square script' writing used today came into common use.

As we examine the acrostics of the Hebrew text, we began to understand the mystery code of ancient Hebrew letters. As we reverse engineer back to original Hebrew letters, we began to see the code revealed in the beautiful alphabet. We then began to drop the vowels, and see the letters came alive. Then, you see the Hebrew Alphabet has the hidden numbering code or Gematria as it termed. While the early Phoenician language alphabet essentially contained the same twenty-two letters, it was not blessed with the same hidden code.

Here is a short, but very illustrative discussion of the mechanics of addition of vowels. See https://en.wikibooks.org/wiki/Hebrew/Introduction/Alphabet#Consonants (accessed 7/21/2016). Granted, for western thought, reading Hebrew is a challenge, but consider how we might read the words **Dn't gv p nw!** if we dropped the vowels in our English texts.

Notes on Vowels

The letters of the Hebrew alphabet are consonantal. Vowels are mostly indicated by markings placed below or above these consonants. In Israel, Modern Hebrew texts are printed without these vowel markings which are often reserved for children's books, poetry, and liturgical pieces. What that means is that the correct pronunciation of every word must be learned and subsequently read from context. At first, this may seem near impossible. However, if you apply this practice to English you will soon realize it is indeed possible to read in such a way.
Dn't gv p nw!

- With vowels: אִמָא

- Without vowels: אימא

There are only five vowel sounds in Modern Hebrew and they are all pronounced fully like Italian. They are: a like in far, e like in less, o like in more, ee like in free, and oo like in food.

****

The ancient Hebrew language with its twenty-two letters was written with a picture, such as an ox, tent, foot or a door. In the master key acrostic of the scriptures (Psalm 119) various organs of the body are referenced: heart, mouth, eyes, hands, feet and mouth—perhaps related to the twenty-two DNA autosomes.

While Aramaic was the everyday language in Jesus' times, Greek was a prominent language and a version of the New Testament was written in Greek—it is crucial to see the difference in translation. The more "western" Greek thought might describe a **pencil** by how it looks, what color is it, what shape it is. In Hebrew thought—what is its function, what does it do? In Greek thought, a **house** is a foundation, roof, and bedrooms. In Hebrew thought, a House is a Home, where family resides and lives.

After Judah went to Babylon, they adopted the Babylonian Aramaic letters, and from then on the Hebrew language has used those Babylonian letters. Ezekiel used the Phoenician alphabet which is letter wise essentially the same as the Hebrew alphabet. Ezekiel's *taw*, written in pre-Babylonian Hebrew, was written as a cross, rather than like the modern letter *taw*. The mark of God, then, was the cross. It was "God's signature." Jesus was nailed on the cross. Ezekiel 9:6 shows a mark (*taw*) is placed on the foreheads of those being sealed in an earlier day. The mark was a sign on the forehead of those who were sealed.

| Strong's <u>226</u> | <u>ō-wt</u> | אוֹת | a sign |

Consider the make-up of the Hebrew letter for the word sign.

1. *alef,* א   the first letter of the alphabet, ox head, yoke, chief, learn
2. *waw,* ו   the sixth letter, a nail, peg or a conjunction, that which joins two things
3. *taw,* ת   the last letter of the alphabet, sign, branded cross, "T"

It is easy to see that the central idea behind the *owt* is the joining, uniting or nailing together of the *alef* and *tav*, or (in Greek), *alpha* and *omega*.

REVELATION 9:4 And it was commanded them that they should not hurt the grass of the earth, neither any green thing, neither any tree; **but only those men which have not the seal of God in their foreheads.**

REVELATION 22:13 I am **Alpha** and **Omega**, the **beginning** and the **end**, the **first** and the **last**.

The *owt* is signifying that we have come into agreement with Him as an Amen people. We agree that He is truly sovereign and has never lost control of the universe, because He planned it from A to Z. Most important, those who are sealed are those who have come into agreement with His plan, those who do not fight against Him, thinking that they have a better idea.

Isaiah spoke of an upper pool by the fuller's field (Isaiah 7:3) and also of a lower pool. Perhaps, trying to find the 'pure' word of God is like a journey from waters that have been muddied by the thoughts of men to the pure waters of the upper pool by the fuller's field—a place of cleansing and whitening in preparation for transfiguration.

ISAIAH 22:9 Ye have seen also the **breaches** of the city of David, that they are many: and **ye gathered together the waters of the lower pool**.

There have been many attempts to reach the upper pool. One such attempt is exploring Hebrew as system of letters based on a verb-based communication. Its concepts are as follows:

> When one begins to look at this dimension, every idea and concept in the scriptures began to communicate a whole new perspective. A verb is an idea in action, it is motion. Again, if we all had common ancestors, then we at one time had a common language. However, most languages in use today are not verb-based. In Hebrew, all words are formed from root words that are comprised of three letters. And these three-letter root words are always verbs. It is emphatically important to know that all words in the original Hebrew Scriptures are formed from three-letter root verbs. This idea and study is mind blowing to those that have studied Greek for years.
>
> Can one understand that all of the ideas and concepts in the Scriptures were trying to communicate to us activity and motion of God? If we could understand and discern the Spiritual Life and idea each verb was emphasizing, we could begin to unlock the simplicity of the Word of God. Since every word is formed from a

three-letter verb, we need to discern the spiritual value of that root verb, the we can begin discerning the simple Spiritual Truth and value of all words in the Hebrew Scriptures. Then the beautiful Hebrew alphabet, and the Hebrew numbering system begins to flow.

EXODUS 31:18 And he gave unto Moses, when he had made an end of communing with him upon mount Sinai, two tables of testimony, tables of stone, **written with the finger of God.**

Many scholars have called the Hebrew alphabet the "Letters of Fire."

11 THE BODY OF CHRIST WORKING TOGETHER

1CORINTHIANS 12:12 **For as the body is one, and hath many members, and all the members of that one body, being many, are one body: so also is Christ.** …
15 If the foot shall say, Because I am not the hand, I am not of the body; is it therefore not of the body?
16 And if the ear shall say, Because I am not the eye, I am not of the body; is it therefore not of the body?
17 If the whole body were an eye, where were the hearing? If the whole were hearing, where were the smelling?
18 **But now hath God set the members every one of them in the body, as it hath pleased him.**

In the Old Testament, Moses went up on the mount and received the pattern of the tabernacle. Then God filled certain workers with wisdom in order to build the various parts of it.

EXODUS 31:2 See, I have called by name Bezaleel the son of Uri, the son of Hur, of the tribe of Judah:
3 And **I have filled him with the spirit of God, in wisdom**, and in understanding, and in knowledge, and **in all manner of workmanship**, …
6 And I, behold, I have given with him Aholiab, the son of Ahisamach, of the tribe of Dan: and in the hearts of all that are wise hearted I have put wisdom, **that they may make all that I have commanded thee;**

Later on David received a pattern for the Lord's house—a pattern so precise, God told him to put in writing and then instruct his son Solomon concerning its construction.

1CHRONICLES 28:19 All this, said David, the **LORD made me understand in writing** by his hand upon me, **even all the works of this pattern.**

20 And David said to Solomon his son, Be strong and of good courage, and do it: fear not, nor be dismayed: for the LORD God, even my God, will be with thee; he will not fail thee, nor forsake thee, **until thou hast finished all the work for the service of the house of the LORD.**

Later on, Jesus and Paul confounded the cloth, brick and mortar concepts by revealing that the tabernacle in the wilderness and the temple built by Solomon were mere symbols of something more profound and much more complex—for they asserted that the true temple was the temple of the human body.

JOHN 2:19 Jesus answered and said unto them, **Destroy this temple, and in three days I will raise it up.**
20 Then said the Jews, Forty and six years was this temple in building, and wilt thou rear it up in three days?
21 **But he spake of the temple of his body.**

1CORINTHIANS 3:16 Know ye not that **ye are the temple of God,** and that the Spirit of God dwelleth in you?

Now, back to the instructions that David received for the temple's construction. David phrased it this way: "… **the LORD made me understand in writing** by his hand upon me, **even all the works of this pattern."** Now, glorious as Solomon's temple was, the human body in its patterns is even more glorious and much more complex. Did you know that David put "in writing" these acrostics: Psalm 9, Psalm 25, Psalm 34, Psalm 37 and Psalm 145? Will we find David's written patterns in these acrostics?

It is no secret that our human temple is beset with ailments and diseases, some are which related to defects in our DNA. Is it possible that we, like Nehemiah, are called to come out of Babylonian captivity and understand the building of the temple of our body? Are secrets of the universe and the temple hidden within acrostic codes in the Bible?

PROVERBS 25:2 **It is the glory of God to conceal a thing**: but the honour of kings is to search out a matter.

PSALMS 139:14 **I will praise thee; for I am fearfully and wonderfully made**: marvellous are thy works; and that my soul knoweth right well.
15 My substance was not hid from thee, when I was made in secret, and curiously wrought in the lowest parts of the earth.
16 Thine eyes did see my substance, yet being unperfect; **and in thy book all my members were written, which in continuance were fashioned, when as yet there was none of them.**

Like in the days of Daniel, there are Christians in this world that have been trained in medicine, science, engineering, computer programming, encryption and all manner of endeavors. However, the Most High has begun to reveal to his people the wisdom hidden from the very foundation of the world. Are there hidden codes in the Bible's acrostics? That is a question we are posing to the body of Christ.

We hope the previous chapters have been appetizers for our readers. In the next chapters, we will serve the meat of the word by providing the main course of the various acrostics we have been able to identify in the scriptures. We invite those, who like Daniel, filled with the Holy Wisdom of God, to come on this journey and may we discover the words, as David wrote**, *in thy book all my members were written.***

קה נֵר־לְרַגְלִי דְבָרֶךָ;   וְאוֹר, לִנְתִיבָתִי.   PSALMS 119:105   NUN נֵ

Thy word is a lamp unto my feet, and a light unto my path.

As we read from the Psalm, the word is a lamp for a path to go forward—and the Most High has given us feet that are to be used for walking on his path. So, we will start presenting one by one in following chapters the acrostic Psalms

12 PSALMS NINE PLUS PSALMS TEN ACROSTICS

The Proverbs 31 acrostic was wonderfully intact and easy to follow. Going from it to the Psalms 9 plus Psalms 10 acrostic is like going from arithmetic to calculus. It is **a broken acrostic thread that spans two chapters** but is presented as only one chapter in the Greek Septuagint translation of the Old Testament.

E.W. Bullinger in Appendix 63 of the *The Companion Bible* describes the Psalm 9 plus the Psalm 10 acrostic:

> "Psalms 9 and 10 are linked together by an Acrostic which, like "the times of trouble" (the great tribulation), of which the two Psalms treat, is purposely broken, and is irregular and out of joint. This Acrostic tells us that the subject of the two Psalms is one, and they are to be connected together."

Note that verse 2 is the beginning of the acrostic. Aleph begins the sentence in verses 2 and 3 and Beth begins the sentence in verse 4, and then the broken thread begins.

Also, bold characters at the beginning of the Hebrew verses correspond to the verse number, so don't confuse the verse number with the character beginning the first Hebrew word in that verse: for example:

Verse 1 = Verse א

In order for our readers to quickly identify the beginning characters of the acrostic, we have preceded it with the hashtag symbol (**#**) which is optically easy to identify within the verse. While we hope that we have properly identified the available threads of the acrostic, we know that it is all too easy to make a mistake and we ask the indulgence of our readers in this matter.

Revealing DNA, Fractal and Quantum Creative Linguistics

[Original background text from http://www.mechon-mamre.org/p/pt/pt2609.htm]

Psalms Chapter 9 תְּהִלִּים

א לַמְנַצֵּחַ, עַל-מוּת לַבֵּן; מִזְמוֹר לְדָוִד.
1 For the Leader; upon Muthlabben. A Psalm of David.

ב # אוֹדֶה יְהוָה, בְּכָל-לִבִּי; # אֲסַפְּרָה, כָּל-נִפְלְאוֹתֶיךָ.
2 I will give thanks unto the LORD with my whole heart; I will tell of all Thy marvellous works. **#Aleph**

ג # אֶשְׂמְחָה וְאֶעֶלְצָה בָךְ; אֲזַמְּרָה שִׁמְךָ עֶלְיוֹן.
3 I will be glad and exult in Thee; I will sing praise to Thy name, O Most High: **#Aleph**

ד # בְּשׁוּב-אוֹיְבַי אָחוֹר; יִכָּשְׁלוּ וְיֹאבְדוּ, מִפָּנֶיךָ.
4 When mine enemies are turned back, they stumble and perish at Thy presence; **#Beth**

ה כִּי-עָשִׂיתָ, מִשְׁפָּטִי וְדִינִי; יָשַׁבְתָּ לְכִסֵּא, שׁוֹפֵט צֶדֶק.
5 For Thou hast maintained my right and my cause; Thou sattest upon the throne as the righteous Judge.

ו # גָּעַרְתָּ גוֹיִם, אִבַּדְתָּ רָשָׁע; שְׁמָם מָחִיתָ, לְעוֹלָם וָעֶד.
6 Thou hast rebuked the nations, Thou hast destroyed the wicked, Thou hast blotted out their name for ever and ever. **#Gimel**

ז הָאוֹיֵב, תַּמּוּ חֳרָבוֹת--לָנֶצַח; וְעָרִים נָתַשְׁתָּ--אָבַד זִכְרָם הֵמָּה.
7 O thou enemy, the waste places are come to an end for ever; and the cities which thou didst uproot, their very memorial is perished.

ח וַיהוָה, לְעוֹלָם יֵשֵׁב; כּוֹנֵן לַמִּשְׁפָּט כִּסְאוֹ.
8 But the LORD is enthroned for ever; He hath established His throne for judgment.

ט וְהוּא, יִשְׁפֹּט-תֵּבֵל בְּצֶדֶק; יָדִין לְאֻמִּים, בְּמֵישָׁרִים.
9 And He will judge the world in righteousness, He will minister judgment to the peoples with equity.

י וִיהִי יְהוָה מִשְׂגָּב לַדָּךְ; מִשְׂגָּב, לְעִתּוֹת בַּצָּרָה.
10 The LORD also will be a high tower for the oppressed, a high tower in times of trouble;

יא וְיִבְטְחוּ בְךָ, יוֹדְעֵי שְׁמֶךָ: כִּי לֹא-עָזַבְתָּ דֹרְשֶׁיךָ יְהוָה.
11 And they that know Thy name will put their trust in Thee; for Thou, LORD, hast not forsaken them that seek Thee.

יב # זַמְּרוּ--לַיהוָה, יֹשֵׁב צִיּוֹן; הַגִּידוּ בָעַמִּים, עֲלִילוֹתָיו.
12 Sing praises to the LORD, who dwelleth in Zion; declare among the peoples His doings. **#Zayin**

Bible Acrostic Code Mysteries

יג כִּי-דֹרֵשׁ דָּמִים, אוֹתָם זָכָר; לֹא-שָׁכַח, צַעֲקַת עניים (עֲנָוִים).	13 For He that avengeth blood hath remembered them; He hath not forgotten the cry of the humble.
יד # חָנְנֵנִי יְהוָה--רְאֵה עָנְיִי, מִשֹּׂנְאָי; מְרוֹמְמִי, מִשַּׁעֲרֵי מָוֶת.	14 Be gracious unto me, O LORD, behold mine affliction at the hands of them that hate me; Thou that liftest me up from the gates of death; **#Heth**
טו לְמַעַן אֲסַפְּרָה, כָּל-תְּהִלָּתֶיךָ: בְּשַׁעֲרֵי בַת-צִיּוֹן--אָגִילָה, בִּישׁוּעָתֶךָ.	15 That I may tell of all Thy praise in the gates of the daughter of Zion, that I may rejoice in Thy salvation.
טז # טָבְעוּ גוֹיִם, בְּשַׁחַת עָשׂוּ; בְּרֶשֶׁת-זוּ טָמָנוּ, נִלְכְּדָה רַגְלָם.	16 The nations are sunk down in the pit that they made; in the net which they hid is their own foot taken. **#Teth**
יז נוֹדַע, # יְהוָה--מִשְׁפָּט עָשָׂה: בְּפֹעַל כַּפָּיו, נוֹקֵשׁ רָשָׁע; הִגָּיוֹן סֶלָה.	17 The LORD hath made Himself known, He hath executed judgment, the wicked is snared in the work of his own hands. Higgaion. Selah **#Yod**
יח יָשׁוּבוּ רְשָׁעִים לִשְׁאוֹלָה: כָּל-גּוֹיִם, שְׁכֵחֵי אֱלֹהִים.	18 The wicked shall return to the nether-world, even all the nations that forget God.
יט כִּי לֹא לָנֶצַח, יִשָּׁכַח אֶבְיוֹן; תִּקְוַת ענוים (עֲנִיִּים), תֹּאבַד לָעַד.	19 For the needy shall not alway be forgotten, nor the expectation of the poor perish for ever.
כ קוּמָה יְהוָה, אַל-יָעֹז אֱנוֹשׁ; יִשָּׁפְטוּ גוֹיִם, עַל-פָּנֶיךָ.	20 Arise, O LORD, let not man prevail; let the nations be judged in Thy sight.
כא שִׁיתָה יְהוָה, מוֹרָה--לָהֶם: יֵדְעוּ גוֹיִם-- אֱנוֹשׁ הֵמָּה סֶּלָה.	21 Set terror over them, O LORD; let the nations know they are but men. Selah **{P}**

Psalms Chapter 10 תְּהִלִּים

א לָמָה יְהוָה, תַּעֲמֹד בְּרָחוֹק; תַּעְלִים, לְעִתּוֹת בַּצָּרָה.	1 Why standest Thou afar off, O LORD? Why hidest Thou Thyself in times of trouble?
ב בְּגַאֲוַת רָשָׁע, יִדְלַק עָנִי; יִתָּפְשׂוּ, בִּמְזִמּוֹת זוּ חָשָׁבוּ.	2 Through the pride of the wicked the poor is hotly pursued, they are taken in the devices that they have imagined.

Revealing DNA, Fractal and Quantum Creative Linguistics

ג # כִּי-הִלֵּל רָשָׁע, עַל-תַּאֲוַת נַפְשׁוֹ; וּבֹצֵעַ בֵּרֵךְ, נִאֵץ יְהוָה.

3 For the wicked boasteth of his heart's desire, and the covetous vaunteth himself, though he contemn the LORD. **#Kaph**

ד רָשָׁע--כְּגֹבַהּ אַפּוֹ, בַּל-יִדְרֹשׁ; אֵין אֱלֹהִים, כָּל-מְזִמּוֹתָיו.

4 The wicked, in the pride of his countenance [, saith]: 'He will not require'; all his thoughts are: 'There is no God.'

ה יָחִילוּ דְרָכָו, בְּכָל-עֵת--מָרוֹם מִשְׁפָּטֶיךָ, מִנֶּגְדּוֹ; כָּל-צוֹרְרָיו, יָפִיחַ בָּהֶם.

5 His ways prosper at all times; Thy judgments are far above out of his sight; as for all his adversaries, he puffeth at them.

ו אָמַר בְּלִבּוֹ, בַּל-אֶמּוֹט; לְדֹר וָדֹר, אֲשֶׁר לֹא-בְרָע.

6 He saith in his heart: 'I shall not be moved, I who to all generations shall not be in adversity.'

ז אָלָה, פִּיהוּ מָלֵא--וּמִרְמוֹת וָתֹךְ; תַּחַת לְשׁוֹנוֹ, עָמָל וָאָוֶן.

7 His mouth is full of cursing and deceit and oppression; under his tongue is mischief and iniquity.

ח יֵשֵׁב, בְּמַאְרַב חֲצֵרִים--בַּמִּסְתָּרִים, יַהֲרֹג נָקִי; עֵינָיו, לְחֵלְכָה יִצְפֹּנוּ.

8 He sitteth in the lurking-places of the villages; in secret places doth he slay the innocent; his eyes are on the watch for the helpless.

ט יֶאֱרֹב בַּמִּסְתָּר, כְּאַרְיֵה בְסֻכֹּה-- יֶאֱרֹב, לַחֲטוֹף עָנִי; {N}
יַחְטֹף עָנִי, בְּמָשְׁכוֹ בְרִשְׁתּוֹ.

9 He lieth in wait in a secret place as a lion in his lair, he lieth in wait to catch the poor; {N}
he doth catch the poor, when he draweth him up in his net.

י ודכה (יִדְכֶּה) יָשֹׁחַ; וְנָפַל בַּעֲצוּמָיו, חלכאים (חֵיל כָּאִים).

10 He croucheth, he boweth down, and the helpless fall into his mighty claws.

יא אָמַר בְּלִבּוֹ, שָׁכַח אֵל; הִסְתִּיר פָּנָיו, בַּל-רָאָה לָנֶצַח.

11 He hath said in his heart: 'God hath forgotten; He hideth His face; He will never see.'

יב # קוּמָה יְהוָה--אֵל, נְשָׂא יָדֶךָ; אַל-תִּשְׁכַּח עניים (עֲנָוִים).

12 Arise, O LORD; O God, lift up Thy hand; forget not the humble. **#Koph**

יג עַל-מֶה, נִאֵץ רָשָׁע אֱלֹהִים; אָמַר בְּלִבּוֹ, לֹא תִדְרֹשׁ.

13 Wherefore doth the wicked contemn God, and say in his heart: 'Thou wilt not require'?

יד # רָאִתָה, כִּי-אַתָּה עָמָל וָכַעַס תַּבִּיט-- לָתֵת בְּיָדֶךָ:

14 Thou hast seen; for Thou beholdest trouble and vexation, to requite them with Thy hand; {N}
unto Thee the helpless committeth himself;

עָלֶיךָ, יַעֲזֹב חֵלְכָה; יָתוֹם, אַתָּה הָיִיתָ עוֹזֵר.	Thou hast been the helper of the fatherless. **#Resh**
טו # שְׁבֹר, זְרוֹעַ רָשָׁע; וָרָע, תִּדְרוֹשׁ-רִשְׁעוֹ בַל-תִּמְצָא.	15 Break Thou the arm of the wicked; and as for the evil man, search out his wickedness, till none be found. **#Shin**
טז יְהוָה מֶלֶךְ, עוֹלָם וָעֶד; אָבְדוּ גוֹיִם, מֵאַרְצוֹ.	16 The LORD is King for ever and ever; the nations are perished out of His land.
יז # תַּאֲוַת עֲנָוִים שָׁמַעְתָּ יְהוָה; תָּכִין לִבָּם, תַּקְשִׁיב אָזְנֶךָ.	17 LORD, Thou hast heard the desire of the humble: Thou wilt direct their heart, Thou wilt cause Thine ear to attend; **#Taw**
יח לִשְׁפֹּט יָתוֹם, וָדָךְ: בַּל-יוֹסִיף עוֹד--לַעֲרֹץ אֱנוֹשׁ, מִן-הָאָרֶץ.	18 To right the fatherless and the oppressed, that man who is of the earth may be terrible no more. **{P}**

13 THE PSALM CHAPTER 25 ACROSTIC

Psalm 25 has a missing letter and one of the other letters is duplicated. In some cases, the letters reside within the same verse. Whether this is by design or due to verses/lines missing from the original, we do not know.

[Original background text from http://www.mechon-mamre.org/p/pt/pt2625.htm]

Psalms Chapter 25 תְּהִלִּים

א לְדָוִד: אֵלֶיךָ יְהוָה, נַפְשִׁי אֶשָּׂא.
1 [A Psalm] of David. Unto Thee, O LORD, do I lift up my soul.

ב # אֱלֹהַי-- # בְּךָ בָטַחְתִּי, אַל-אֵבוֹשָׁה; אַל-יַעַלְצוּ אֹיְבַי לִי.
2 O my God, in Thee have I trusted, let me not be ashamed; let not mine enemies triumph over me. **#Aleph & #Beth**

ג # גַּם כָּל-קֹוֶיךָ, לֹא יֵבֹשׁוּ; יֵבֹשׁוּ, הַבּוֹגְדִים רֵיקָם.
3 Yea, none that wait for Thee shall be ashamed; they shall be ashamed that deal treacherously without cause. **#Gimel**

ד # דְּרָכֶיךָ יְהוָה, הוֹדִיעֵנִי; אֹרְחוֹתֶיךָ לַמְּדֵנִי.
4 Show me Thy ways, O LORD; teach me Thy paths. **#Daleth**

ה # הַדְרִיכֵנִי בַאֲמִתֶּךָ, # וְלַמְּדֵנִי-- כִּי-אַתָּה, אֱלֹהֵי יִשְׁעִי; אוֹתְךָ קִוִּיתִי, כָּל-הַיּוֹם.
5 Guide me in Thy truth, and teach me; for Thou art the God of my salvation; {N}
for Thee do I wait all the day. **#Hey & #Waw**

ו # זְכֹר-רַחֲמֶיךָ יְהוָה, וַחֲסָדֶיךָ: כִּי מֵעוֹלָם הֵמָּה.
6 Remember, O LORD, Thy compassions and Thy mercies; for they have been from of old. **#Zayin**

Bible Acrostic Code Mysteries

ז # חַטֹּאות נְעוּרַי, וּפְשָׁעַי-- אַל-תִּזְכֹּר: כְּחַסְדְּךָ זְכָר-לִי-אַתָּה-- לְמַעַן טוּבְךָ יְהוָה.

7 Remember not the sins of my youth, nor my transgressions; {N} according to Thy mercy remember Thou me, for Thy goodness' sake, O LORD. **#Heth**

ח # טוֹב-וְיָשָׁר יְהוָה; עַל-כֵּן יוֹרֶה חַטָּאִים בַּדָּרֶךְ.

8 Good and upright is the LORD; therefore doth He instruct sinners in the way. **#Teth**

ט # יַדְרֵךְ עֲנָוִים, בַּמִּשְׁפָּט; וִילַמֵּד עֲנָוִים דַּרְכּוֹ.

9 He guideth the humble in justice; and He teacheth the humble His way. **#Yod**

י # כָּל-אָרְחוֹת יְהוָה, חֶסֶד וֶאֱמֶת-- לְנֹצְרֵי בְרִיתוֹ, וְעֵדֹתָיו.

10 All the paths of the LORD are mercy and truth unto such as keep His covenant and His testimonies. **#Kaph**

יא # לְמַעַן-שִׁמְךָ יְהוָה; וְסָלַחְתָּ לַעֲוֹנִי, כִּי רַב-הוּא.

11 For Thy name's sake, O LORD, pardon mine iniquity, for it is great. **#Lamed**

יב # מִי-זֶה הָאִישׁ, יְרֵא יְהוָה-- יוֹרֶנּוּ, בְּדֶרֶךְ יִבְחָר.

12 What man is he that feareth the LORD? Him will He instruct in the way that he should choose. **#Mem**

יג # נַפְשׁוֹ, בְּטוֹב תָּלִין; וְזַרְעוֹ, יִירַשׁ אָרֶץ.

13 His soul shall abide in prosperity; and his seed shall inherit the land. **#Nun**

יד # סוֹד יְהוָה, לִירֵאָיו; וּבְרִיתוֹ, לְהוֹדִיעָם.

14 The counsel of the LORD is with them that fear Him; and His covenant, to make them know it. **#Samek**

טו # עֵינַי תָּמִיד, אֶל-יְהוָה: כִּי הוּא-יוֹצִיא מֵרֶשֶׁת רַגְלָי.

15 Mine eyes are ever toward the LORD; for He will bring forth my feet out of the net. **#Ayin**

טז # פְּנֵה-אֵלַי וְחָנֵּנִי: כִּי-יָחִיד וְעָנִי אָנִי.

16 Turn Thee unto me, and be gracious unto me; for I am solitary and afflicted. **#Pey**

KOPH ק MISSING AND RESH ך DUPLICATED

יח # רְאֵה עָנְיִי, וַעֲמָלִי; וְשָׂא, לְכָל-חַטֹּאותָי.

18 See mine affliction and my travail; and forgive all my sins. **#Resh**

יט # רְאֵה-אֹיְבַי כִּי-רָבּוּ; וְשִׂנְאַת חָמָס שְׂנֵאוּנִי.

19 Consider how many are mine enemies, and the cruel hatred wherewith they hate me. **#Resh**

כ # שָׁמְרָה נַפְשִׁי, וְהַצִּילֵנִי;   אַל-אֵבוֹשׁ, כִּי-חָסִיתִי בָךְ.   20 O keep my soul, and deliver me; let me not be ashamed, for I have taken refuge in Thee. **#Shin**

כא # תֹּם-וָיֹשֶׁר יִצְּרוּנִי: כִּי, קִוִּיתִיךָ.   21 Let integrity and uprightness preserve me, because I wait for Thee. **#Taw**

כב פְּדֵה אֱלֹהִים, אֶת-יִשְׂרָאֵל–   מִכֹּל, צָרוֹתָיו.   22 Redeem Israel, O God, out of all his troubles. **{P}**

14 THE PSALM CHAPTER 34 ACROSTIC

There are 23 verses in this chapter and the acrostic starts with verse 2.

[Original background text from http://www.mechon-mamre.org/p/pt/pt2634.htm]

Psalms Chapter 34 תְּהִלִּים

א לְדָוִד-- בְּשַׁנּוֹתוֹ אֶת-טַעְמוֹ, לִפְנֵי אֲבִימֶלֶךְ; וַיְגָרְשֵׁהוּ, וַיֵּלַךְ.

1 [A Psalm] of David; when he changed his demeanour before Abimelech, who drove him away, and he departed.

ב # אֲבָרְכָה אֶת-יְהוָה בְּכָל-עֵת; תָּמִיד, תְּהִלָּתוֹ בְּפִי.

2 I will bless the LORD at all times; His praise shall continually be in my mouth. **#Aleph**

ג # בַּיהוָה, תִּתְהַלֵּל נַפְשִׁי; יִשְׁמְעוּ עֲנָוִים וְיִשְׂמָחוּ.

3 My soul shall glory in the LORD; the humble shall hear thereof, and be glad. **#Beth**

ד # גַּדְּלוּ לַיהוָה אִתִּי; וּנְרוֹמְמָה שְׁמוֹ יַחְדָּו.

4 O magnify the LORD with me, and let us exalt His name together. **#Gimel**

ה # דָּרַשְׁתִּי אֶת-יְהוָה וְעָנָנִי; # וּמִכָּל-מְגוּרוֹתַי הִצִּילָנִי.

5 I sought the LORD, and He answered me, and delivered me from all my fears. **#Daleth**

ו # הִבִּיטוּ אֵלָיו וְנָהָרוּ; # וּפְנֵיהֶם, אַל-יֶחְפָּרוּ.

6 They looked unto Him, and were radiant; and their faces shall never be abashed. **#Hey** & **#Waw**

7 This poor man cried, and the LORD heard, and saved him out of all his troubles. **#Zayin**	ז # זֶה עָנִי קָרָא, וַיהוָה שָׁמֵעַ; וּמִכָּל-צָרוֹתָיו, הוֹשִׁיעוֹ.
8 The angel of the LORD encampeth round about them that fear Him, and delivereth them. **#Heth**	ח # חֹנֶה מַלְאַךְ-יְהוָה סָבִיב לִירֵאָיו; וַיְחַלְּצֵם.
9 O consider and see that the LORD is good; happy is the man that taketh refuge in Him. **#Teth**	ט # טַעֲמוּ וּרְאוּ, כִּי-טוֹב יְהוָה; אַשְׁרֵי הַגֶּבֶר, יֶחֱסֶה-בּוֹ.
10 O fear the LORD, ye His holy ones; for there is no want to them that fear Him. **#Yod**	י # יְראוּ אֶת-יְהוָה קְדֹשָׁיו: כִּי-אֵין מַחְסוֹר, לִירֵאָיו.
11 The young lions do lack, and suffer hunger; but they that seek the LORD want not any good thing. **#Kaph**	יא # כְּפִירִים, רָשׁוּ וְרָעֵבוּ; וְדֹרְשֵׁי יְהוָה, לֹא-יַחְסְרוּ כָל-טוֹב.
12 Come, ye children, hearken unto me; I will teach you the fear of the LORD. **#Lamed**	יב # לְכוּ-בָנִים, שִׁמְעוּ-לִי; יִרְאַת יְהוָה, אֲלַמֶּדְכֶם.
13 Who is the man that desireth life, and loveth days, that he may see good therein? **#Mem**	יג # מִי-הָאִישׁ, הֶחָפֵץ חַיִּים; אֹהֵב יָמִים, לִרְאוֹת טוֹב.
14 Keep thy tongue from evil, and thy lips from speaking guile. **#Nun**	יד # נְצֹר לְשׁוֹנְךָ מֵרָע; וּשְׂפָתֶיךָ, מִדַּבֵּר מִרְמָה.
15 Depart from evil, and do good; seek peace, and pursue it. **#Samek**	טו # סוּר מֵרָע, וַעֲשֵׂה-טוֹב; בַּקֵּשׁ שָׁלוֹם וְרָדְפֵהוּ.
16 The eyes of the LORD are toward the righteous, and His ears are open unto their cry. **#Ayin**	טז # עֵינֵי יְהוָה, אֶל-צַדִּיקִים; וְאָזְנָיו, אֶל-שַׁוְעָתָם.
17 The face of the LORD is against them that do evil, to cut off the remembrance of them from the earth. **#Pey**	יז # פְּנֵי יְהוָה, בְּעֹשֵׂי רָע; לְהַכְרִית מֵאֶרֶץ זִכְרָם.
18 They cried, and the LORD heard, and delivered them out of all their troubles. **#Tsade**	יח # צָעֲקוּ, וַיהוָה שָׁמֵעַ; וּמִכָּל-צָרוֹתָם, הִצִּילָם.

יט # קָרוֹב יְהוָה, לְנִשְׁבְּרֵי-לֵב; וְאֶת-דַּכְּאֵי-רוּחַ יוֹשִׁיעַ.	**19** The LORD is nigh unto them that are of a broken heart, and saveth such as are of a contrite spirit. **#Koph**
כ # רַבּוֹת, רָעוֹת צַדִּיק; וּמִכֻּלָּם, יַצִּילֶנּוּ יְהוָה.	**20** Many are the ills of the righteous, but the LORD delivereth him out of them all. **#Resh**
כא # שֹׁמֵר כָּל-עַצְמוֹתָיו; אַחַת מֵהֵנָּה, לֹא נִשְׁבָּרָה.	**21** He keepeth all his bones; not one of them is broken. **#Shin**
כב # תְּמוֹתֵת רָשָׁע רָעָה; וְשֹׂנְאֵי צַדִּיק יֶאְשָׁמוּ.	**22** Evil shall kill the wicked; and they that hate the righteous shall be held guilty. **#Taw**
כג פֹּדֶה יְהוָה, נֶפֶשׁ עֲבָדָיו; וְלֹא יֶאְשְׁמוּ, כָּל-הַחֹסִים בּוֹ.	**23** The LORD redeemeth the soul of His servants; and none of them that take refuge in Him shall be desolate. **{P}**

15 THE PSALM CHAPTER 37 ACROSTIC

Bullinger's comments on this Psalm are as follows:

> "In this Psalm, the series is perfect and complete. Every letter has two verses of two lines each, except three: vv. 7 … (…, Daleth=D), 20 (…, Kaph=K), and 34 (…, Koph=K)"

The use of the letter "K" in the above quotation is perhaps a bit confusing, however the letters referenced are Daleth, Kaph and Koph. Unlike some of the other acrostics we have examined, the same character can appear multiple times within the same English verse. Perhaps the English translation could be better viewed in quadruplet sentences.

[Original background text from http://www.mechon-mamre.org/p/pt/pt2637.htm]

Psalms Chapter 37 תְּהִלִּים

א לְדָוִד: # אַל-תִּתְחַר בַּמְּרֵעִים; # אַל-תְּקַנֵּא, בְּעֹשֵׂי עַוְלָה.

1 [A Psalm] of David. Fret not thyself because of evil-doers, neither be thou envious against them that work unrighteousness. **#Aleph**

ב כִּי כֶחָצִיר, מְהֵרָה יִמָּלוּ; וּכְיֶרֶק דֶּשֶׁא, יִבּוֹלוּן.

2 For they shall soon wither like the grass, and fade as the green herb.

ג # בְּטַח בַּיהוָה, וַעֲשֵׂה-טוֹב; שְׁכָן-אֶרֶץ, וּרְעֵה אֱמוּנָה.

3 Trust in the LORD, and do good; dwell in the land, and cherish faithfulness. **#Beth**

ד וְהִתְעַנַּג עַל-יְהוָה; וְיִתֶּן-לְךָ, מִשְׁאֲלֹת לִבֶּךָ.

4 So shalt thou delight thyself in the LORD; and He shall give thee the petitions of thy heart.

Bible Acrostic Code Mysteries

ה # גּוֹל עַל-יְהוָה דַּרְכֶּךָ; וּבְטַח עָלָיו, וְהוּא יַעֲשֶׂה.	5 Commit thy way unto the LORD; trust also in Him, and He will bring it to pass. **#Gimel**
ו וְהוֹצִיא כָאוֹר צִדְקֶךָ; וּמִשְׁפָּטֶךָ, כַּצָּהֳרָיִם.	6 And He will make thy righteousness to go forth as the light, and thy right as the noonday.
ז # דּוֹם, לַיהוָה-- וְהִתְחוֹלֵל-לוֹ: אַל-תִּתְחַר, בְּמַצְלִיחַ דַּרְכּוֹ; בְּאִישׁ, עֹשֶׂה מְזִמּוֹת.	7 Resign thyself unto the LORD, and wait patiently for Him; {N} fret not thyself because of him who prospereth in his way, because of the man who bringeth wicked devices to pass. **#Daleth**
ח # הֶרֶף מֵאַף, וַעֲזֹב חֵמָה; אַל-תִּתְחַר, אַךְ-לְהָרֵעַ.	8 Cease from anger, and forsake wrath; fret not thyself, it tendeth only to evil-doing. **#Hey**
ט כִּי-מְרֵעִים, יִכָּרֵתוּן; וְקֹוֵי יְהוָה, הֵמָּה יִירְשׁוּ-אָרֶץ.	9 For evil-doers shall be cut off; but those that wait for the LORD, they shall inherit the land.
י # וְעוֹד מְעַט, וְאֵין רָשָׁע; וְהִתְבּוֹנַנְתָּ עַל-מְקוֹמוֹ וְאֵינֶנּוּ.	10 And yet a little while, and the wicked is no more; yea, thou shalt look well at his place, and he is not. **#Waw**
יא וַעֲנָוִים יִירְשׁוּ-אָרֶץ; וְהִתְעַנְּגוּ, עַל-רֹב שָׁלוֹם.	11 But the humble shall inherit the land, and delight themselves in the abundance of peace.
יב # זֹמֵם רָשָׁע, לַצַּדִּיק; וְחֹרֵק עָלָיו שִׁנָּיו.	12 The wicked plotteth against the righteous, and gnasheth at him with his teeth. **#Zayin**
יג אֲדֹנָי יִשְׂחַק-לוֹ: כִּי-רָאָה, כִּי-יָבֹא יוֹמוֹ.	13 The Lord doth laugh at him; for He seeth that his day is coming.
יד חֶרֶב, פָּתְחוּ רְשָׁעִים-- וְדָרְכוּ קַשְׁתָּם: לְהַפִּיל, עָנִי וְאֶבְיוֹן; לִטְבוֹחַ, יִשְׁרֵי-דָרֶךְ.	14 The wicked have drawn out the sword, and have bent their bow; {N} to cast down the poor and needy, to slay such as are upright in the way;
טו # חַרְבָּם, תָּבוֹא בְלִבָּם; וְקַשְּׁתוֹתָם, תִּשָּׁבַרְנָה.	15 Their sword shall enter into their own heart, and their bows shall be broken. **#Heth**
טז # טוֹב-מְעַט, לַצַּדִּיק-- מֵהֲמוֹן, רְשָׁעִים רַבִּים.	16 Better is a little that the righteous hath than the abundance of many wicked. **#Teth**

יז כִּי זְרוֹעוֹת רְשָׁעִים, תִּשָּׁבַרְנָה; וְסוֹמֵךְ צַדִּיקִים יְהוָה.	17 For the arms of the wicked shall be broken; but the LORD upholdeth the righteous.
יח # יוֹדֵעַ יְהוָה, יְמֵי תְמִימִם; וְנַחֲלָתָם, לְעוֹלָם תִּהְיֶה.	18 The LORD knoweth the days of them that are wholehearted; and their inheritance shall be for ever. **#Yod**
יט לֹא-יֵבֹשׁוּ, בְּעֵת רָעָה; וּבִימֵי רְעָבוֹן יִשְׂבָּעוּ.	19 They shall not be ashamed in the time of evil; and in the days of famine they shall be satisfied.
כ # כִּי רְשָׁעִים, יֹאבֵדוּ, וְאֹיְבֵי יְהוָה, # כִּיקַר כָּרִים; # כָּלוּ בֶעָשָׁן כָּלוּ.	20 For the wicked shall perish, and the enemies of the LORD shall be as the fat of lambs--they shall pass away in smoke, they shall pass away. **#Kaph**
כא # לֹוֶה רָשָׁע, וְלֹא יְשַׁלֵּם; וְצַדִּיק, חוֹנֵן וְנוֹתֵן.	21 The wicked borroweth, and payeth not; but the righteous dealeth graciously, and giveth. **#Lamed**
כב כִּי מְבֹרָכָיו, יִירְשׁוּ אָרֶץ; וּמְקֻלָּלָיו, יִכָּרֵתוּ.	22 For such as are blessed of Him shall inherit the land; and they that are cursed of Him shall be cut off.
כג # מֵיְהוָה, מִצְעֲדֵי-גֶבֶר כּוֹנָנוּ; וְדַרְכּוֹ יֶחְפָּץ.	23 It is of the LORD that a man's goings are established; and He delighted in his way. **#Mem**
כד כִּי-יִפֹּל לֹא-יוּטָל: כִּי-יְהוָה, סוֹמֵךְ יָדוֹ.	24 Though he fall, he shall not be utterly cast down; for the LORD upholdeth his hand.
כה # נַעַר, הָיִיתִי-- גַּם-זָקַנְתִּי: וְלֹא-רָאִיתִי, צַדִּיק נֶעֱזָב; וְזַרְעוֹ, מְבַקֶּשׁ-לָחֶם.	25 I have been young, and now am old; {N} yet have I not seen the righteous forsaken, nor his seed begging bread. **#Nun**
כו כָּל-הַיּוֹם, חוֹנֵן וּמַלְוֶה; וְזַרְעוֹ, לִבְרָכָה.	26 All the day long he dealeth graciously, and lendeth; and his seed is blessed.
כז # סוּר מֵרָע, וַעֲשֵׂה-טוֹב; וּשְׁכֹן לְעוֹלָם.	27 Depart from evil, and do good; and dwell for evermore. **#Samek**
כח כִּי יְהוָה, אֹהֵב מִשְׁפָּט, וְלֹא-יַעֲזֹב אֶת-חֲסִידָיו, לְעוֹלָם נִשְׁמָרוּ; וְזֶרַע רְשָׁעִים נִכְרָת.	28 For the LORD loveth justice, and forsaketh not His saints; they are preserved for ever; {N} but the seed of the wicked shall be cut off.
כט # צַדִּיקִים יִירְשׁוּ-אָרֶץ; וְיִשְׁכְּנוּ לָעַד	29 The righteous shall inherit the land, and dwell therein for ever. **#Ayin**

עָלֶיהָ.

ל # פִּי־צַדִּיק, יֶהְגֶּה חָכְמָה; וּלְשׁוֹנוֹ, תְּדַבֵּר מִשְׁפָּט.

30 The mouth of the righteous uttereth wisdom, and his tongue speaketh justice. **#Pey**

לא תּוֹרַת אֱלֹהָיו בְּלִבּוֹ; לֹא תִמְעַד אֲשֻׁרָיו.

31 The law of his God is in his heart; none of his steps slide.

לב # צוֹפֶה רָשָׁע, לַצַּדִּיק; וּמְבַקֵּשׁ, לַהֲמִיתוֹ.

32 The wicked watcheth the righteous, and seeketh to slay him. **#Tsade**

לג יְהוָה, # לֹא־יַעַזְבֶנּוּ בְיָדוֹ; וְלֹא יַרְשִׁיעֶנּוּ, בְּהִשָּׁפְטוֹ.

33 The LORD will not leave him in his hand, nor suffer him to be condemned when he is judged.

לד # קַוֵּה אֶל־יְהוָה, וּשְׁמֹר דַּרְכּוֹ, וִירוֹמִמְךָ, לָרֶשֶׁת אָרֶץ; בְּהִכָּרֵת רְשָׁעִים תִּרְאֶה.

34 Wait for the LORD, and keep His way, and He will exalt thee to inherit the land; {N}
when the wicked are cut off, thou shalt see it. **#Koph**

לה # רָאִיתִי, רָשָׁע עָרִיץ; וּמִתְעָרֶה, כְּאֶזְרָח רַעֲנָן.

35 I have seen the wicked in great power, and spreading himself like a leafy tree in its native soil. **#Resh**

לו וַיַּעֲבֹר, וְהִנֵּה אֵינֶנּוּ; וָאֲבַקְשֵׁהוּ, וְלֹא נִמְצָא.

36 But one passed by, and, lo, he was not; yea, I sought him, but he could not be found.

לז # שְׁמָר־תָּם, וּרְאֵה יָשָׁר: כִּי־אַחֲרִית לְאִישׁ שָׁלוֹם.

37 Mark the man of integrity, and behold the upright; for there is a future for the man of peace. **#Shin**

לח וּפֹשְׁעִים, נִשְׁמְדוּ יַחְדָּו; אַחֲרִית רְשָׁעִים נִכְרָתָה.

38 But transgressors shall be destroyed together; the future of the wicked shall be cut off.

לט וּתְשׁוּעַת צַדִּיקִים, מֵיְהוָה; # מָעוּזָּם, בְּעֵת צָרָה.

39 But the salvation of the righteous is of the LORD; He is their stronghold in the time of trouble. **#Taw**

מ וַיַּעְזְרֵם יְהוָה, וַיְפַלְּטֵם: יְפַלְּטֵם מֵרְשָׁעִים, וְיוֹשִׁיעֵם--כִּי־חָסוּ בוֹ.

40 And the LORD helpeth them, and delivereth them; He delivereth them from the wicked, and saveth them, because they have taken refuge in Him. {P}

16 THE PSALMS 111 & 112 ACROSTIC

Bullinger has pretty much identical comments about Psalm 111 and Psalm 112.

> "Psalm 111, In this Psalm the series is perfect and complete. The Psalm has twenty-two lines, each line commencing with successive letters of the alphabet.
>
> Psalm 112 is formed on the model of Psalm 111, the two Psalms forming a pair[2]; Psalm 111 being occupied with Jehovah and Psalm 112 being occupied with the man that revereth Jehovah.
>
> 2 With the further peculiarity that the first three verses in each Psalm consist of two portions: the last two of three portions."

The two Psalms are therefore presented together in this chapter.

[Original background text from http://www.mechon-mamre.org/p/pt/pt26b1.htm]

Psalms Chapter 111 מִתְהִלֵּי

א הַלְלוּ-יָהּ:
אוֹדֶה יְהוָה, # בְּכָל-לֵבָב; # בְּסוֹד יְשָׁרִים וְעֵדָה.

1 Hallelujah. {N}
I will give thanks unto the LORD with my whole heart, in the council of the upright, and in the congregation. **#Aleph&Beth**

ב # גְּדֹלִים, מַעֲשֵׂי יְהוָה; # דְּרוּשִׁים, לְכָל-חֶפְצֵיהֶם.

2 The works of the LORD are great, sought out of all them that have delight therein. **#Gimel&Daleth**

ג # הוֹד-וְהָדָר פָּעֳלוֹ; # וְצִדְקָתוֹ, עֹמֶדֶת לָעַד.

3 His work is glory and majesty; and His righteousness endureth for ever. **#Hey&Waw**

Bible Acrostic Code Mysteries

ד # זֵכֶר עָשָׂה, לְנִפְלְאוֹתָיו; # חַנּוּן וְרַחוּם יְהוָה.

4 He hath made a memorial for His wonderful works; the LORD is gracious and full of compassion. **#Zayin&Heth**

ה # טֶרֶף, נָתַן לִירֵאָיו; # יִזְכֹּר לְעוֹלָם בְּרִיתוֹ.

5 He hath given food unto them that fear Him; He will ever be mindful of His covenant. **#Teth&Yod**

ו # כֹּחַ מַעֲשָׂיו, הִגִּיד לְעַמּוֹ-- # לָתֵת לָהֶם, נַחֲלַת גּוֹיִם.

6 He hath declared to His people the power of His works, in giving them the heritage of the nations. **#Kaph&Lamed**

ז # מַעֲשֵׂי יָדָיו, אֱמֶת וּמִשְׁפָּט; # נֶאֱמָנִים, כָּל-פִּקּוּדָיו.

7 The works of His hands are truth and justice; all His precepts are sure. **#Mem&Nun**

ח # סְמוּכִים לָעַד לְעוֹלָם; # עֲשׂוּיִם, בֶּאֱמֶת וְיָשָׁר.

8 They are established for ever and ever, they are done in truth and uprightness. **#Samek&Ayin**

ט # פְּדוּת, שָׁלַח לְעַמּוֹ-- # צִוָּה-לְעוֹלָם בְּרִיתוֹ; קָדוֹשׁ וְנוֹרָא שְׁמוֹ.

9 He hath sent redemption unto His people; He hath commanded His covenant for ever; Holy and awful is His name. **#Pey&Tsade**

י # רֵאשִׁית חָכְמָה, יִרְאַת יְהוָה-- # שֵׂכֶל טוֹב, לְכָל-עֹשֵׂיהֶם; # תְּהִלָּתוֹ, עֹמֶדֶת לָעַד.

10 The fear of the LORD is the beginning of wisdom; a good understanding have all they that do thereafter; His praise endureth for ever. **#Shin&Taw**

[Original background text from http://www.mechon-mamre.org/p/pt/pt26b2.htm]

Psalms Chapter 112 תְּהִלִּים

א הַלְלוּ-יָהּ:
אַשְׁרֵי-אִישׁ, יָרֵא אֶת-יְהוָה;
בְּמִצְוֹתָיו, חָפֵץ מְאֹד.

1 Hallelujah. {N}
Happy is the man that feareth the LORD, that delighteth greatly in His commandments. **#Aleph&Beth**

ב # גִּבּוֹר בָּאָרֶץ, יִהְיֶה זַרְעוֹ; # דּוֹר יְשָׁרִים יְבֹרָךְ.

2 His seed shall be mighty upon earth; the generation of the upright shall be blessed. **#Gimel&Daleth**

ג # הוֹן-וָעֹשֶׁר בְּבֵיתוֹ; # וְצִדְקָתוֹ, עֹמֶדֶת לָעַד.

3 Wealth and riches are in his house; and his merit endureth for ever. **Hey&Waw**

ד # זָרַח בַּחֹשֶׁךְ אוֹר, לַיְשָׁרִים; # חַנּוּן וְרַחוּם וְצַדִּיק.	**4** Unto the upright He shineth as a light in the darkness, gracious, and full of compassion, and righteous. **#Zayin&Heth**
ה # טוֹב-אִישׁ, חוֹנֵן וּמַלְוֶה; # יְכַלְכֵּל דְּבָרָיו בְּמִשְׁפָּט.	**5** Well is it with the man that dealeth graciously and lendeth, that ordereth his affairs rightfully. **#Teth&Yod**
ו # כִּי-לְעוֹלָם לֹא-יִמּוֹט; # לְזֵכֶר עוֹלָם, יִהְיֶה צַדִּיק.	**6** For he shall never be moved; the righteous shall be had in everlasting remembrance. **#Kaph&Lamed**
ז # מִשְּׁמוּעָה רָעָה, לֹא יִירָא; # נָכוֹן לִבּוֹ, בָּטֻחַ בַּיהוָה.	**7** He shall not be afraid of evil tidings; his heart is stedfast, trusting in the LORD. **#Mem&Nun**
ח # סָמוּךְ לִבּוֹ, לֹא יִירָא; # עַד אֲשֶׁר-יִרְאֶה בְצָרָיו.	**8** His heart is established, he shall not be afraid, until he gaze upon his adversaries. **#Samek&Ayin**
ט # פִּזַּר, נָתַן לָאֶבְיוֹנִים-- # צִדְקָתוֹ, עֹמֶדֶת לָעַד; קַרְנוֹ, תָּרוּם בְּכָבוֹד.	**9** He hath scattered abroad, he hath given to the needy; his righteousness endureth for ever; his horn shall be exalted in honour. **#Pey&Tsade**
י רָשָׁע יִרְאֶה, וְכָעָס-- # שִׁנָּיו יַחֲרֹק וְנָמָס; # תַּאֲוַת רְשָׁעִים תֹּאבֵד.	**10** The wicked shall see it, and be vexed; he shall gnash with his teeth, and melt away; **{N}** the desire of the wicked shall perish. **{P}** **#Shin&Taw**

17 OPENING THE PSALM 119 MATRIX

NUMBERS 3:12 And I, behold, I have taken the Levites from among the children of Israel instead of all **the firstborn that openeth the matrix** among the children of Israel: therefore the Levites shall be mine;

HEBREWS 12:22 But, ye came to Mount Zion, and to a city of the living God, to the heavenly Jerusalem, and **to myriads of messengers**,
23 to the company and assembly of **the first-born in heaven enrolled**, and to God the judge of all, and to spirits of righteous men made perfect,
24 and to **a mediator of a new covenant - Jesus**, and to blood of sprinkling, speaking better things than that of Abel! (YLT Version).

Jesus was preferentially concerned with the tabernacle of our body and also with the body of believers. A myriad is 20,000 consisting of two sets of 10,000. He is the fairest of 10,000 sons. While this is a rich subject in its own right, we simply direct our readers to follow-up by reading Psalm 68:17, Jude 14 and Song of Solomon 5:10 & 6:13 and leave it at that.

Is Psalm 119 a matrix of creative letters and words that form the very foundation of our existence? **Definition**. A **matrix** is a rectangular array of numbers or other mathematical objects for which operations such as addition and multiplication are defined.

The diagrams on a page are presented in two dimensions and we can readily grasp the four seen dimensions of length, width, depth and time. However, think of a rectangular array of data points. The 1980's and 90's saw widespread use of relational computer programs such as Excel and Basic—it then became possible to process huge amounts of data. In Basic each data point could have ten dimensions (internal sets of data) assigned to it. And then the overall data point itself constituted the eleventh dimension. Just handling the four seen dimensions is quite enough to occupy our mind, but perhaps when the **matrix of our spiritual mind** is fully opened, we will comprehend the four seen dimensions along with the seven unseen dimensions now being probed by scientists.

We have discussed the acrostic nature of Psalm 119 and its structure of eight verses for each of the twenty-two letters of the Hebrew alphabet in earlier chapters 7 and 8. Early estimates by scientists of the number of transcribed genes were in the range of 100,000 and then as refinements were made it came down to 50,000 and eventually to the present estimate of around 21,000. We have briefly looked at the Hebrew numbering system and wondered out loud if a relationship exists between it and the number of genes. Maybe, maybe not, but we never know what gems and nuggets exist in the ground unless we mine them.

It has been said that in actuality, we exist as just a bunch of numbers in a holographic world. Or, perhaps in string theory, we are a bundle of vibrating strings. But, on the other hand, these numbers, or strings as it may be, are uniquely configured and we are, as the psalmist wrote, *fearfully and wonderfully made.*

A very succinct article on the use of DNA to store digital information was recently published.

Scientists work toward storing digital information in DNA

Monday, July 25, 2016; By MALCOLM RITTTER ~ Associated Press; NEW YORK

He begins the article by discussing how a Microsoft employee is researching the possibility of storing digital data in DNA. The problem of yesterday's data reading technology such as tape readers and floppy discs being outmoded is discussed. And then, after a period of time, the actual substrate on which the information is stored begins to deteriorate. Here is an excerpt from the article:

> "DNA is by its essence an information-storing molecule; the genes we pass from generation to generation transmit the blueprints for creating the human body. That information is stored in strings of what's often called the four-letter DNA code. That really refers to sequences of four building blocks -- abbreviated as A, C, T and G -- found in the DNA molecule.
>
> Specific sequences give the body directions for creating particular proteins. Digital devices, on the other hand, store information in a two-letter code that produces strings of ones and zeroes. A capital "A," for example, is 01000001. Converting digital information to DNA involves translating between the two codes. In one lab, for example, a capital A can become ATATG. The idea is once that transformation is made, strings of DNA can be custom-made to carry the new code, and hence the information that code contains.
>
> One selling point is durability. Scientists can recover and read DNA sequences from fossils of Neanderthals and even older life forms.
>
> So as a storage medium, "it could last thousands and thousands of years," said Luis Ceze of the University of Washington, who works with Microsoft on DNA data storage.

Advocates also stress DNA crams information into very little space. Almost every cell of your body carries about six feet of it; that adds up to billions of miles in a single person.

In terms of information storage, that compactness could mean storing all the publicly accessible data on the internet in a space the size of a shoebox, Ceze said. In fact, all the digital information in the world might be stored in a load of whitish, powdery DNA that fits in space the size of a large van, said Nick Goldman of the European Bioinformatics Institute in Hinxton, England."

****

The previous article discusses how digital information might be translated from the binary code into the A-T and G-C configurations of DNA. This then brings up a very logical question. The overall pattern of the twenty-two letters and eight verse acrostic sets seems to flow with the overarching pattern of DNA. What would we get, if we translated the acrostic words into numbers and compared the numbers with DNA patterns?

Up to this point, we have presented both the English translation and the Hebrew with vowel markings side by side. However, this book could just as easily been written in Portuguese, Russian, Mandarin or any number of languages. When it comes to numbers, we need to strip away all languages other than Hebrew and use the Hebrew constants as written in their early form.

Very frankly, we feel that we are opening a door to a matrix and we have little idea what we might find. So, we will simply dip our toe into the water and use an excel spreadsheet to look at the first eight verses of Psalm 119 and how the letters might translate into numbers.

TOTAL			26	1008	130	1100	511
VERSE	119	1	יהוה:	בתורת	ההלכים	תמימי־דרך	אשרי

1 Blessed are the undefiled in the way, who walk in the law of the LORD.

TOTAL			719	84	684	350	511
VERSE	119	2	ידרשוהו:	בכל־לב	עדתיו	נצרי	אשרי
			568	84	474	340	511

2 Blessed are they that keep his testimonies, and that seek him with the whole heart.

TOTAL			255	436	305	411	101
VERSE	119	3	הלכו:	בדרכיו	עולה	לא־פעלו	אף

3 They also do no iniquity: they walk in his ways.

TOTAL			45	570	694	605	436
VERSE	119	4	מאד:	לשמר	פקדיך	צויתה	אתה

4 Thou hast commanded us to keep thy precepts diligently.

TOTAL			118	570	234	233	49
VERSE	119	5	חקיך:	לשמר	דרכי	יכנו	אחלי

5 O that my ways were directed to keep thy statutes!

TOTAL				1291	38	534	8
VERSE	119	6	אֶל־כָּל־מִצְוֺתֶיךָ׃	בְּהַבִּיטִי	לֹא־אֵבוֹשׁ	אָז

6 Then shall I not be ashamed, when I have respect unto all thy commandments

TOTAL			694	439	86	34	512	515
VERSE	119	7	צִדְקֶךָ׃	מִשְׁפְּטֵי	בְּלָמְדִי	לֵבָב	בְּיֹשֶׁר	אוֹדְךָ

7 I will praise thee with uprightness of heart, when I shall have learned thy righteous judgments.

TOTAL				119	523	541	1019
VERSE	119	8	עַד־מְאֹד׃	אַל־תַּעַזְבֵנִי	אֶשְׁמֹר	אֶת־חֻקֶּיךָ

8 I will keep thy statutes: O forsake me not utterly.

Below is the very crude template of the spreadsheet that we used. We are hopeful that those in the body of Christ who are very skilled in processing large amounts of data and uncovering hidden relationships (such as fractals) will join our quest to understand the meaning and beauty of acrostics.

Letter	NUM	LET.	VALUE	VALUE	VALUE	VALUE	VALUE
ALEPH	1	א	0	0	0	0	1
BETH	2	ב	0	2	0	0	0
GIMEL	3	ג	0	0	0	0	0
DALETH	4	ד	0	0	0	0	0
HEY	5	ה	10	0	10	0	0
WAW	6	ו, ּו	6	6	0	0	0
ZAYIN	7	ז	0	0	0	0	0
HETH	8	ח	0	0	0	0	0
TETH	9	ט	0	0	0	0	0
YOD	10	י	10	0	10	20	10
KAPH	20	כ	0	0	20	0	0
LAMED	30	ל	0	0	30	0	0
MEM	40	מ	0	0	0	80	0
NUN	50	נ	0	0	0	0	0
SAMEK	60	ס, ם	0	0	60	0	0
AYIN	70	ע	0	0	0	0	0
PEY	80	פ	0	0	0	0	0
TSADE	90	צ	0	0	0	0	0
KOPH	100	ק	0	0	0	0	0
RESH	200	ר	0	200	0	600	200
SHIN	300	ש	0	0	0	0	300
TAW	400	ת	0	800	0	400	0
TOTAL			26	1008	130	1100	511
VERSE	119	1	יְהוָה׃	בְּתוֹרַת	הַהֹלְכִים	תְּמִימֵי־דָרֶךְ	אַשְׁרֵי

Bible Acrostic Code Mysteries

The codes for putting the Hebrew alphabet into the computer for cross comparison with DNA coding already exist: For example for **Aleph**: **Character** א [Unicode: Decimal 1488 and Hex U+05D0] [UTF-8: Decimal 215 144 and Hex D7 90] UTF-16 Dec 1488 & Hex 05D0] Numeric character reference: [Dec 㢘 Hex &#x5D0].

18 PSALM 145 ACROSTIC

Bullinger wrote this note about Psalm 145.

> "In the Psalm the Acrostic is perfect, with the exception of the letter … (*Nun*=N), which should come between vv. 13 and 14. … Through the infirmity of some transcriber, the verse was probably omitted by him. It must have been in the more ancient manuscripts, because it is preserved in the ancient Versions: viz. The Sept., Syr, Arabic, Ethiopic and Vulgate."

[Original background text from http://www.mechon-mamre.org/p/pt/pt26e5.htm]

Psalms Chapter 145 תְּהִלִּים

א # תְּהִלָּה, לְדָוִד:
אֲרוֹמִמְךָ אֱלוֹהַי הַמֶּלֶךְ;   וַאֲבָרְכָה שִׁמְךָ, לְעוֹלָם וָעֶד.

1 [A Psalm of] praise; of David. **{N}**
I will **extol** Thee, my God, O King; and I will bless Thy name for ever and ever. **#Aleph**

ב # בְּכָל-יוֹם אֲבָרְכֶךָּ;   וַאֲהַלְלָה שִׁמְךָ, לְעוֹלָם וָעֶד.

2 Every day will I bless Thee; and I will praise Thy name for ever and ever. **#Beth**

ג # גָּדוֹל יְהוָה וּמְהֻלָּל מְאֹד;   וְלִגְדֻלָּתוֹ, אֵין חֵקֶר.

3 Great is the LORD, and highly to be praised; and His greatness is unsearchable. **#Gimel**

ד # דּוֹר לְדוֹר, יְשַׁבַּח מַעֲשֶׂיךָ;   וּגְבוּרֹתֶיךָ יַגִּידוּ.

4 One **generation** shall laud Thy works to another, and shall declare Thy mighty acts. **#Daleth**

Bible Acrostic Code Mysteries

ה # הֲדַר, כְּבוֹד הוֹדֶךָ-- וְדִבְרֵי נִפְלְאֹתֶיךָ אָשִׂיחָה.

5 The glorious **splendour** of Thy majesty, and Thy wondrous works, will I rehearse. **#Hey**

ו # וֶעֱזוּז נוֹרְאֹתֶיךָ יֹאמֵרוּ; וגדלותיך (וּגְדֻלָּתְךָ) אֲסַפְּרֶנָּה.

6 And men shall speak of the **might** of Thy tremendous acts; and I will tell of Thy greatness. **#Waw**

ז # זֵכֶר רַב-טוּבְךָ יַבִּיעוּ; וְצִדְקָתְךָ יְרַנֵּנוּ.

7 They shall utter the **fame** of Thy great goodness, and shall sing of Thy righteousness. **#Zayin**

ח # חַנּוּן וְרַחוּם יְהוָה; אֶרֶךְ אַפַּיִם, וּגְדָל-חָסֶד.

8 The LORD is **gracious**, and full of compassion; slow to anger, and of great mercy. **#Heth**

ט # טוֹב-יְהוָה לַכֹּל; וְרַחֲמָיו, עַל-כָּל-מַעֲשָׂיו.

9 The LORD is **good** to all; and His tender mercies are over all His works. **#Teth**

י # יוֹדוּךָ יְהוָה, כָּל-מַעֲשֶׂיךָ; וַחֲסִידֶיךָ, יְבָרְכוּכָה..

10 All Thy works shall **praise** Thee, O LORD; and Thy saints shall bless Thee. **#Yod**

יא # כְּבוֹד מַלְכוּתְךָ יֹאמֵרוּ; וּגְבוּרָתְךָ יְדַבֵּרוּ.

11 They shall speak of the **glory** of Thy kingdom, and talk of Thy might; **#Kaph**

יב # לְהוֹדִיעַ, לִבְנֵי הָאָדָם-- גְּבוּרֹתָיו; וּכְבוֹד, הֲדַר מַלְכוּתוֹ.

12 To **make known** to the sons of men His mighty acts, and the glory of the majesty of His kingdom. **#Lamed**

יג # מַלְכוּתְךָ, מַלְכוּת כָּל-עֹלָמִים; וּמֶמְשַׁלְתְּךָ, בְּכָל-דּוֹר וָדֹר.

13 Thy **kingdom** is a kingdom for all ages, and Thy dominion endureth throughout all generations. **#Mem**

LETTER NUN נ MISSING

יד # סוֹמֵךְ יְהוָה, לְכָל-הַנֹּפְלִים; וְזוֹקֵף, לְכָל-הַכְּפוּפִים.

14 The LORD **upholdeth** all that fall, and raiseth up all those that are bowed down. **#Samek**

טו # עֵינֵי-כֹל, אֵלֶיךָ יְשַׂבֵּרוּ; וְאַתָּה נוֹתֵן-לָהֶם אֶת-אָכְלָם בְּעִתּוֹ.

15 The **eyes** of all wait for Thee, and Thou givest them their food in due season. **#Ayin**

טז # פּוֹתֵחַ אֶת-יָדֶךָ; וּמַשְׂבִּיעַ

16 Thou **openest** Thy hand, and satisfiest every living thing with favour. **#Pey**

לְכָל-חַי רָצוֹן.

יז # צַדִּיק יְהוָה, בְּכָל-דְּרָכָיו; וְחָסִיד, בְּכָל-מַעֲשָׂיו.

17 The LORD is **righteous** in all His ways, and gracious in all His works. **#Tsade**

יח # קָרוֹב יְהוָה, לְכָל-קֹרְאָיו— לְכֹל אֲשֶׁר יִקְרָאֻהוּ בֶאֱמֶת.

18 The LORD is **nigh** unto all them that call upon Him, to all that call upon Him in truth. **#Koph**

יט # רְצוֹן-יְרֵאָיו יַעֲשֶׂה; וְאֶת-שַׁוְעָתָם יִשְׁמַע, וְיוֹשִׁיעֵם.

19 He will fulfil the **desire** of them that fear Him; He also will hear their cry, and will save them. **#Resh**

כ # שׁוֹמֵר יְהוָה, אֶת-כָּל-אֹהֲבָיו; וְאֵת כָּל-הָרְשָׁעִים יַשְׁמִיד.

20 The LORD **preserveth** all them that love Him; but all the wicked will He destroy. **#Shin**

כא # תְּהִלַּת יְהוָה, יְדַבֶּר-פִּי: וִיבָרֵךְ כָּל-בָּשָׂר, שֵׁם קָדְשׁוֹ—לְעוֹלָם וָעֶד.

21 My mouth shall speak the **praise** of the LORD; and let all flesh bless His holy name for ever and ever. **#Taw**

19 LAMENTATIONS ACROSTICS

Lamentations, as you might guess by its name, is not a cheerful book. But, it does have a unique structure that is almost similar to the seven lamped Hebrew candlestick. However, using this pattern, it would have only five lamps rather than seven.

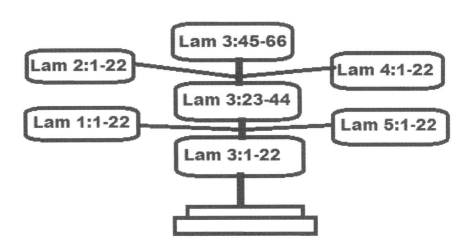

Fig. 19.1 A representation of the structure of Lamentations.

The first and second chapters of Lamentations are twenty-two verse acrostics. The third chapter is unique in that it has three verse sets of the twenty-two Hebrew characters. The fourth chapter has a twenty-two verse acrostic. The fifth chapter is not an acrostic, but it does preserve the twenty-two verse pattern.

We have long suspected that the twenty-two character acrostic nature of Lamentations had something to do with DNA defects. However, we recently found these scriptures which is like a trail of 'bread crumbs' leading to that conclusion.

EZEKIEL 19:10 Thy mother is like a **vine in thy blood**, planted by the waters: **she was fruitful and full of branches by reason of many waters.**
11 And she had **strong rods for the sceptres of them that bare rule**, and her stature was exalted among the thick branches, and she appeared in her height with the multitude of her branches.
12 But she was plucked up in fury, she was cast down to the ground, and the east wind dried up her fruit: **her strong rods were broken and withered; the fire consumed them.**
13 And now she is planted in the wilderness, in a dry and thirsty ground.
14 **And fire is gone out of a rod of her branches,** which hath devoured her fruit, so that **she hath no strong rod to be a sceptre** to rule. **This is a lamentation**, and shall be for a **lamentation.**

The *vine in thy blood* and the *strong rods were broken* and withered are a major clue that mutations, additions and/or subtractions in the DNA are a **lamentation**. And then the word **lamentation** is doubled for emphasis.

Let's take a brief at the structure Lamentations Chapter three to inspect how the acrostic in this sixty-six verse chapter unfolds. Remember that the first Hebrew symbol is the **verse number** and not the beginning of verse itself. The acrostic is in sets of three—for example three Alephs and then three Beths.

[Original background text from http://www.mechon-mamre.org/p/pt/pt3203.htm]

Lamentations Chapter 3 אֵיכָה

א אֲנִי הַגֶּבֶר רָאָה עֳנִי, בְּשֵׁבֶט עֶבְרָתוֹ.
1 I am the man that hath seen affliction by the rod of His wrath.

ב אוֹתִי נָהַג וַיֹּלַךְ, חֹשֶׁךְ וְלֹא-אוֹר.
2 He hath led me and caused me to walk in darkness and not in light.

ג אַךְ בִּי יָשֻׁב יַהֲפֹךְ יָדוֹ, כָּל-הַיּוֹם. {ס}
3 Surely against me He turneth His hand again and again all the day. {S}

ד בִּלָּה בְשָׂרִי וְעוֹרִי, שִׁבַּר עַצְמוֹתָי.
4 My flesh and my skin hath He worn out; He hath broken my bones.

ה בָּנָה עָלַי וַיַּקַּף, רֹאשׁ וּתְלָאָה.
5 He hath builded against me, and compassed me with gall and travail.

ו בְּמַחֲשַׁכִּים הוֹשִׁיבַנִי, כְּמֵתֵי עוֹלָם. {ס}
6 He hath made me to dwell in dark places, as those that have been long dead. {S}

ז גָּדַר בַּעֲדִי וְלֹא אֵצֵא, הִכְבִּיד נְחָשְׁתִּי.	7 He hath hedged me about, that I cannot go forth; He hath made my chain heavy.
ח גַּם כִּי אֶזְעַק וַאֲשַׁוֵּעַ, שָׂתַם תְּפִלָּתִי.	8 Yea, when I cry and call for help, He shutteth out my prayer.
ט גָּדַר דְּרָכַי בְּגָזִית, נְתִיבֹתַי עִוָּה. {ס}	9 He hath enclosed my ways with hewn stone, He hath made my paths crooked. {S}

From inspection of the previous verses, the pattern is easily discerned. Verses 1-3 start with ALEPH, verses 4-6 start with BETH, and verses 7-9 start with GIMEL … and verses 63-66 start with TAW. And one can observe, that the message conveyed by chapter 3 is extremely gloomy.

Scientists have found that only a low percentage of the DNA substance actually makes proteins. The remaining part was called "junk DNA" because it seemed to serve no purpose. However, gradually purpose have begun to be found and some scientists have changed the term to "dark DNA"—implying that full knowledge about what it really does has not yet been brought to light. A discussion of this change in attitude is given in the following article *Mysterious Noncoding DNA: 'Junk' or Genetic Power Player?* from an email by Jenny Marder[13], November 7, 2011 at 4:03 PM EDT from this website (accessed 6/30/2016)
http://www.pbs.org/newshour/rundown/junk-dna/

"Genes represent only a tiny fraction — 1 percent — of our overall genetic material. Then there's the other 99 percent of our DNA — the stuff that doesn't make protein.

This swath of the genome was once considered "junk," and though a good deal of it is still believed to be nonfunctional, it is now more respectfully referred to as "noncoding DNA." It is still largely an unexplored wilderness — disorderly and mysterious, but researchers have found that some of this noncoding DNA is in fact essential to how our genes function and plays a role in how we look, how we act and the diseases that afflict us.

Embedded in this 99 percent is DNA responsible for the mechanics of gene behavior: regulatory DNA. Greg Wray of Duke University's Institute for Genome Sciences and Policy describes the regulatory DNA as the software for our genes, a set of instructions that tells the genome how to use the traditional coding genes.

"It's like a recipe book," Wray said. "It tells you how to make the meal. You need to know the amounts. You need to know the order. The noncoding DNA tells you how much to make, when to make it and under what circumstances."

Transcription factors — proteins that bind to DNA sequences — function like a sort of molecular switch. Shaped like tiny Pac-Mans with clefts, they attach to stretches of noncoding DNA and modulate whether the gene will be turned on or off, whether it will function and how much protein it will produce."

****

We want to consider the possibility that encoded somewhere in the acrostic are numerical patterns of defects that are prevalent in the coding or non-coding genes of the human DNA.

The key to the defects perhaps goes all the way back to the garden where certain transactions took place regarding the eye and the mouth.

GENESIS 3:5 For God doth know that in the day ye eat thereof, then **your eyes shall be opened**, and ye shall be as gods, knowing good and evil.
6 And when the woman saw that the tree was good for food, and that it was **pleasant to the eyes**, and a tree to be desired to make one wise, she took of the fruit thereof, **and did eat**, and gave also unto her husband with her; and **he did eat**.
7 And **the eyes of them both were opened**, and they knew that they were naked; and they sewed fig leaves together, and made themselves aprons.
8 And they heard the voice of the LORD God walking in the garden in the cool of the day: and Adam and his wife hid themselves from the presence of the LORD God amongst the trees of the garden.

Jeremiah is widely acknowledged to be the author of Lamentations and we do not think that he would insert an intentional defect into the acrostic structure unless he were moved by the Spirit to do it. So, he wrote the first chapter of Lamentations in the form of a perfect acrostic. Here is an excerpt from verses 16 and 17 of chapter 1.

[Original background text from http://www.mechon-mamre.org/p/pt/pt3201.htm]

Lamentations Chapter 1 אֵיכָה

טז עַל-אֵלֶּה אֲנִי בוֹכִיָּה, עֵינִי עֵינִי יֹרְדָה מַּיִם--כִּי-רָחַק מִמֶּנִּי מְנַחֵם, מֵשִׁיב נַפְשִׁי; הָיוּ בָנַי שׁוֹמֵמִים, כִּי גָבַר אוֹיֵב. {ס}

16 'For these things I weep; **mine eye, mine eye** runneth down with water; because the comforter is far from me, even he that should refresh my soul; my children are desolate, because the enemy hath prevailed.' {S} **Ayin**

יז פֵּרְשָׂה צִיּוֹן בְּיָדֶיהָ, אֵין מְנַחֵם לָהּ-- צִוָּה יְהוָה לְיַעֲקֹב, סְבִיבָיו צָרָיו; הָיְתָה יְרוּשָׁלַם לְנִדָּה, בֵּינֵיהֶם. {ס}

17 Zion spreadeth forth her hands; there is none to comfort her; the LORD hath **commanded** concerning Jacob, that they that are round about him should be his adversaries; Jerusalem is among them as one unclean. {S} **Pe**

Ayin ע – the 16th letter name is derived from Proto-Semitic *ʿayn- "eye", and the Phoenician letter had an eye-shape.

Fig. 19.2 Hebrew symbols for Ayin and Pe

Pe פ – the 17th letter name means mouth, to speak, a word.

Inspection of Lamentations chapter 1 shows that **Ayin** is in its expected position in the 16th verse and **Pe** is in its expected position in the 17th verse. Therefore, Jeremiah knew his alphabet. But, do you think it is possible that he might later make multiple mistakes – not only in chapter 2, but also in chapters 3 and 4? Let's find out.

Lamentations Chapter 2 אֵיכָה

טז פָּצוּ עָלַיִךְ פִּיהֶם, כָּל-אֹיְבַיִךְ--שָׁרְקוּ וַיַּחַרְקוּ-שֵׁן, אָמְרוּ בִּלָּעְנוּ; אַךְ זֶה הַיּוֹם שֶׁקִּוִּינֻהוּ, מָצָאנוּ רָאִינוּ. {ס}

16 All thine enemies have opened their **mouth** wide against thee; they hiss and gnash the **teeth**; they say: 'We have swallowed her up; certainly this is the day that we looked for; we have found, we have **seen** it.' {S}

יז עָשָׂה יְהוָה אֲשֶׁר זָמָם, בִּצַּע אֶמְרָתוֹ אֲשֶׁר צִוָּה מִימֵי-קֶדֶם--הָרַס, וְלֹא חָמָל; וַיְשַׂמַּח עָלַיִךְ אוֹיֵב, הֵרִים קֶרֶן צָרָיִךְ. {ס}

17 The LORD hath done that which He devised; He hath performed His word that He **commanded** in the days of old; He hath thrown down unsparingly; and He hath caused the enemy to rejoice over thee, He hath exalted the horn of thine adversaries. {S}

Why is the position of **Pe** and **Ayin** reversed? Ayin should be in position 16. Has the **mouth** eating the forbidden fruit taken precedence over the **spiritual vision eye**? Well, maybe Jeremiah just made a mistake—perhaps he was just tired that day.

Lamentations Chapter 3 אֵיכָה

מח פַּלְגֵי-מַיִם תֵּרַד עֵינִי, עַל-שֶׁבֶר בַּת-עַמִּי. {ס}

48 Mine **eye** runneth down with rivers of water, for the breach of the daughter of my people. {S}

מט עֵינִי נִגְּרָה וְלֹא תִדְמֶה, מֵאֵין הֲפֻגוֹת.

49 Mine **eye** is poured out, and ceaseth not, without any intermission,

The same thing happened in chapter 3, **Pe** was placed before **Ayin**. In chapter three, each letter is an acrostic for **three** verses. Forty-eight divided by three gives the **16th** position where **Ayin** should have been. Did Jeremiah make more 'mistakes?'

Lamentations Chapter 4 אֵיכָה

טז פְּנֵי יְהוָה חִלְּקָם, לֹא יוֹסִיף לְהַבִּיטָם; פְּנֵי כֹהֲנִים לֹא נָשָׂאוּ, זְקֵנִים (וּזְקֵנִים) לֹא חָנָנוּ. {ס}

16 The anger of the LORD hath divided them; He will no more regard them; they respected not the persons of the priests, they were not gracious unto the elders. {S}

יז עוֹדֵינָה (עוֹדֵינוּ) תִּכְלֶינָה עֵינֵינוּ, אֶל-עֶזְרָתֵנוּ הָבֶל; בְּצִפִּיָּתֵנוּ צִפִּינוּ, אֶל-גּוֹי לֹא יוֹשִׁעַ. {ס}

17 As for us, our **eyes** do yet fail for our vain help; in our **watching** we have **watched** for a nation that could not save. {S}

The same thing happens in chapter 4. Clearly, the inversion of the mouth **Pe** over the eye **Ayin** in chapters 2, 3 and 4 was intentional. Is this the wrench that was thrown into the DNA gears because of man's disobedience? It would seem that Lamentations would be a very rich field for data mining.

20 THE ESTHER ACROSTIC

Bullinger, in his Appendix 60, discusses that many have observed that no Divine Name or Title is found in the book of Esther. He suggests the reason for this has been the disobedience of God's people and God has hidden his face from them. However, he identifies five acrostic instances where the Divine Name is embedded in code form. For example, Bullinger identifies the Tetragrammon name being spelled coded backward (anti-sense direction) in Esther 1:20 but it is spelled forward in a subsequent verse. The Esther acrostic presentation is somewhat veiled in that, rather than using lines, it uses the front and back letters of certain key words.

When RNA receives its coding from DNA, the coding takes place in what is called an **anti-sense** direction to the **sense** direction. Without getting technical about it, just think of a row of books and on the left side is a book end named **Three** and on the right side is a book end named **Five**. For example, the coding section of DNA has a '**3 book end**' and then has intervening coding until it reaches a '**5 book end**." On the other hand, RNA starts with the '**5 book end**' and collects intervening coding until it reaches the '**3 book end**.'

YHWH is often used as a mnemonic for the name of the LORD. The Hebrew letters involved are Yod-Hey-Waw-Hey as shown in the enlarged type for the word LORD in the texts which will follow. For one initially reading the Hebrew letters, Yod can be a little tricky in that it looks like an apostrophe punctuation mark. Waw is sometimes capitalized so that it is presented similar to the English I. However, like the lower case English **i**, when Waw is in lower case, it looks more like a slightly tilted seven. Note the YHWH in the first Bible verse mentioning the LORD. The Hebrew letters are enlarged and bolded so that it is easy to find the Yod-Hey-Waw-Hey.

Revealing DNA, Fractal and Quantum Creative Linguistics

[Original background text from http://www.mechon-mamre.org/p/pt/pt0102.htm)

Genesis Chapter 1 בְּרֵאשִׁית

ד אֵלֶּה תוֹלְדוֹת הַשָּׁמַיִם וְהָאָרֶץ, בְּהִבָּרְאָם: בְּיוֹם, עֲשׂוֹת יְהוָה אֱלֹהִים--אֶרֶץ וְשָׁמָיִם.

4 These are the generations of the heaven and of the earth when they were created, in the day that the **LORD** God made earth and heaven. **YHWH**

In Esther 1:20 the Divine Name is given in reverse as reflecting the controversy between Queen Vashti and the King.

[Original background text from http://www.mechon-mamre.org/p/pt/pt3301.htm and following chapters]

Esther Chapter 1 אֶסְתֵּר

כ וְנִשְׁמַע פִּתְגָם הַמֶּלֶךְ אֲשֶׁר-יַעֲשֶׂה בְּכָל-מַלְכוּתוֹ, כִּי רַבָּה הִיא; וְכָל-הַנָּשִׁים, יִתְּנוּ יְקָר לְבַעְלֵיהֶן--לְמִגָּדוֹל, וְעַד-קָטָן.

20 And when the king's decree which he shall make shall be published throughout all his kingdom, great though **it be, all the wives will give** to their husbands honour, both to great and small.' **HWHY**

However, when Esther begins to act, God reveals himself in Esther 5:4 in the characters in proper order in Esther 5:4. But, for Haman in verse 13, the embedded code is hidden in the anti-sense direction.

Esther Chapter 5 אֶסְתֵּר

ד וַתֹּאמֶר אֶסְתֵּר, אִם-עַל-הַמֶּלֶךְ טוֹב-- יָבוֹא הַמֶּלֶךְ וְהָמָן הַיּוֹם, אֶל-הַמִּשְׁתֶּה אֲשֶׁר-עָשִׂיתִי לוֹ.

4 And Esther said: 'If it seem good unto the king, **let the king and Haman come this day** unto the banquet that I have prepared for him.'

YHWH

יג וְכָל-זֶה, אֵינֶנּוּ שֹׁוֶה לִי: בְּכָל-עֵת, אֲשֶׁר אֲנִי רֹאֶה אֶת-מָרְדֳּכַי הַיְּהוּדִי--יוֹשֵׁב, בְּשַׁעַר הַמֶּלֶךְ.

13 Yet all **this availeth me nothing**, so long as I see Mordecai the Jew sitting at the king's gate.'

HWHY

Then, in Esther 7:7, the Tetragrammon is spelled forward because God is now ruling. And, just previously, in verse 5, the name of the I AM אֶהְיֶה is revealed.

Esther Chapter 7 אֶסְתֵּר

ה וַיֹּאמֶר הַמֶּלֶךְ אֲחַשְׁוֵרוֹשׁ, וַיֹּאמֶר לְאֶסְתֵּר הַמַּלְכָּה: מִי ה**וּא** זֶ**ה** וְאֵ**י**-זֶ**ה** הוּא, אֲשֶׁר-מְלָאוֹ לִבּוֹ לַעֲשׂוֹת כֵּן.

7:5 Then spoke the king Ahasuerus and said unto Esther the queen: **'Who is he, and where is he, that durst presume in his heart to do so?'**
I AM

ז וְהַמֶּלֶךְ קָם בַּחֲמָתוֹ, מִמִּשְׁתֵּה הַיַּיִן, אֶל-גִּנַּת, הַבִּיתָן; וְהָמָן עָמַד, לְבַקֵּשׁ עַל-נַפְשׁוֹ מֵאֶסְתֵּר הַמַּלְכָּה--כִּי רָאָה, כִּ**י**-כָלְתָ**ה** אֵלָי**ו** הָרָעָ**ה** מֵאֵת הַמֶּלֶךְ.

7:7 And the king arose in his wrath from the banquet of wine and went into the palace garden; but Haman remained to make request for his life to Esther the queen; for he saw **that there was evil determined against him** by the king.

YHWH

And, who is this I AM? His name is revealed in Exodus Chapter 3 and He is the **Aleph and Taw**, or perhaps we should say in more familiar terms, **I am the Alpha and Omega, I am the Light of the World** and **I am the way, the truth and the life**. For Yeshua the Christ said that **I am the beginning and the end**.

JOHN 8:58 Jesus said unto them, Verily, verily, I say unto you, **Before** Abraham was, **I am**.

See the I AM in Hebrew occurring twice in the following verse.

[Original background text from http://www.mechon-mamre.org/p/pt/pt0203.htm]

Exodus Chapter 3 שְׁמוֹת

יד וַיֹּאמֶר אֱלֹהִים אֶל-מֹשֶׁה, **אֶהְיֶה** אֲשֶׁר **אֶהְיֶה**; וַיֹּאמֶר, כֹּה תֹאמַר לִבְנֵי יִשְׂרָאֵל, אֶהְיֶה, שְׁלָחַנִי אֲלֵיכֶם.

14 And God said unto Moses: **'I AM THAT I AM'**; and He said: 'Thus shalt thou say unto the children of Israel: I AM hath sent me unto you.'

21 FROM NAHUM'S ACROSTIC TO TELEPATHY

We have previously quoted this information in Chapter 9 from J.A. Motyer:

"Nahum 1: 1- 9 The Aleph covers three lines. There seems to be an interjection of 2 lines before the rest of the consonants, which covers only one verse each. The letter zayin appears in the second position of the line."

****

This acrostic is very broken and the letters that we have highlighted are mostly guesses. Previous writers examining these scriptures seem to have had the same difficulties. However, in the interest of completeness in presenting Bible acrostics, we include it here.

[Original background text from http://www.mechon-mamre.org/p/pt/pt1901.htm]

Nahum Chapter 1 נחום

א מַשָּׂא, נִינְוֵה--סֵפֶר חֲזוֹן נַחוּם, הָאֶלְקֹשִׁי.

1 The burden of Nineveh. The book of the vision of Nahum the Elkoshite.

ב **אֵל** קַנּוֹא וְנֹקֵם יְהוָה, נֹקֵם יְהוָה וּבַעַל חֵמָה; נֹקֵם יְהוָה לְצָרָיו, וְנוֹטֵר הוּא לְאֹיְבָיו.

2 The LORD is a jealous and avenging God, the LORD avengeth and is full of wrath; the LORD taketh vengeance on His adversaries, and He reserveth wrath for His enemies. **ALEPH**

ג יְהוָה, אֶרֶךְ אַפַּיִם וגדול- (וּגְדָל-) כֹּחַ, וְנַקֵּה, לֹא יְנַקֶּה; יְהוָה, בְּ**סוּפָה** וּבִשְׂעָרָה דַּרְכּוֹ, וְעָנָן, אֲבַק רַגְלָיו.

3 The LORD is long-suffering, and great in power, and will by no means clear the guilty; the LORD, in the whirlwind and in the storm is His way, and the clouds are the dust of His feet. **BETH**

Bible Acrostic Code Mysteries

ד **גּ**וֹעֵר בַּיָּם וַיַּבְּשֵׁהוּ, וְכָל-הַנְּהָרוֹת
הֶחֱרִיב; אֻמְלַל בָּשָׁן וְכַרְמֶל, וּפֶרַח
לְבָנוֹן אֻמְלָל.

4 He rebuketh the sea, and maketh it dry, and drieth up all the rivers; Bashan languisheth, and Carmel, and the flower of Lebanon languisheth. **GIMEL&HEY**

ה הָרִים רָעֲשׁוּ מִמֶּנּוּ, וְהַגְּבָעוֹת
הִתְמֹגָגוּ; וַתִּשָּׂא הָאָרֶץ מִפָּנָיו, וְתֵבֵל וְכָל-
יֹשְׁבֵי בָהּ.

5 The mountains quake at Him, and the hills melt; and the earth is upheaved at His presence, yea, the world, and all that dwell therein. **WAW**

ו לִפְנֵי **ז**ַעְמוֹ מִי יַעֲמוֹד, וּמִי יָקוּם בַּחֲרוֹן
אַפּוֹ; חֲמָתוֹ נִתְּכָה כָאֵשׁ, וְהַצֻּרִים נִתְּצוּ מִמֶּנּוּ.

6 Who can stand before His indignation? And who can abide in the fierceness of His anger? His fury is poured out like fire, and the rocks are broken asunder before Him. **ZAYIN**

ז טוֹב יְהוָה, לְמָעוֹז בְּיוֹם צָרָה; וְיֹדֵעַ, חֹסֵי
בוֹ.

7 The LORD is good, a stronghold in the day of trouble; and He knoweth them that take refuge in Him.

ח וּבְשֶׁטֶף עֹבֵר, כָּלָה יַעֲשֶׂה מְקוֹמָהּ;
וְאֹיְבָיו, יְרַדֶּף-חֹשֶׁךְ.

8 But with an overrunning flood He will make a full end of the place thereof, and darkness shall pursue His enemies.

ט **מַ**ה-תְּחַשְּׁבוּן, אֶל-יְהוָה--כָּלָה, הוּא
עֹשֶׂה; לֹא-תָקוּם פַּעֲמַיִם, צָרָה.

9 What do ye devise against the LORD? He will make a full end; trouble shall not rise up the second time. **TAW**

Christians have relied on the printed word of the scriptures, and rightly so, because it opens a door of learning about the attributes of God. And, amazingly—as proven by the Dead Sea scrolls, the written word has been remarkably preserved over the years. However, a more important goal is to have the printed word become the Living Word within our hearts.

2 CORINTHIANS 3:2 Ye are our epistle **written in our hearts**, known and read of all men:
3 Forasmuch as ye are manifestly declared to be the epistle of Christ ministered by us, **written not with ink, but with the Spirit of the living God**; not in tables of stone, **but in fleshy tables of the heart.**

The path to spiritual maturity begins with identifying the symbols and their parables, and then learning the truths that these symbols represent. The Hebrews at times worshipped a symbol rather than understanding the majesty of God represented by that symbol.

NUMBERS 21:9 And Moses made a serpent of brass, and put it upon a pole, and it came to pass, that if a serpent had bitten any man, **when he beheld the serpent of brass, he lived**.

2KINGS 18:4 He removed the high places, and **brake the images**, and cut down the groves, and brake in pieces the **brasen serpent** that Moses had made: for unto those days the children of Israel did burn incense to it: and he called it **Nehushtan**.

The study of the tabernacle and the temple revealed wonderful truths, but these were only symbols of the true spiritual reality. In a way, it became a **Nehushtan** to the Jews when they ignored the truth it represented.

MARK 14:58 We heard him say, I will destroy this temple that is made with hands, and within three days **I will build another made without hands**.

Another example is the Mazzaroth with its twelve star constellation symbols revealed in Job chapters 38 and 39. But, it was perverted to become and **then worshipped as a system of prediction rather than seeking answers directly from the Spirit of God**. At times and places, God has intervened by providing his people with wonderful technology that was far above the existing norm. Consider what was revealed to Benjamin and Joseph in terms of the GPS technology of today.

GENESIS 44:11 Then they speedily took down every man his sack to the ground, and opened every man his sack.
12 And he searched, and began at the eldest, and left at the youngest: and **the cup was found in Benjamin's sack.**

You well know the story of Joseph and the treachery of his brothers. However, more details are given in ***The Book of Jasher***— referenced twice in the Bible (see Joshua 10:13 and II Samuel 1:18). See online http://www.sacred-texts.com/chr/apo/jasher/index.htm. The story goes that Joseph met with Benjamin privately and showed him a map of the stars and asked him where his brother Joseph was. Later, a cup was placed in Benjamin's sack which basically was a tracker for Benjamin's journey.

JASHER 53:18 And he ordered them to bring before him **his map of the stars, whereby Joseph knew all the times**, and Joseph said unto Benjamin, I have heard that the Hebrews are acquainted with all wisdom, dost thou know anything of this?
19 And Benjamin said, Thy servant is knowing also in all the wisdom which my father taught me, and Joseph said unto Benjamin, **Look now at this instrument and understand where thy brother Joseph is in Egypt, who you said went down to Egypt**.
20 And Benjamin beheld that instrument with the map of the stars of heaven, and he was wise and looked therein to know where his brother was, and Benjamin divided the whole land of Egypt into four divisions, **and he found that he who was sitting upon the throne before him was his brother Joseph**, and Benjamin wondered greatly, and when Joseph saw that his brother Benjamin was so much astonished, he said unto Benjamin, What hast thou seen, and why art thou astonished?
21 **And Benjamin said unto Joseph, I can see by this that Joseph my brother sitteth here with me upon the throne**, and Joseph said unto him, I am Joseph thy brother, reveal

not this thing unto thy brethren; behold I will send thee with them when they go away, and I will command them to be brought back again into the city, and I will take thee away from them.

Of course, man's GPS is puny compared to the GPS of the One who spread out the heavens—however, Daniel did say that **at the time of the end: many shall run to and fro, and knowledge shall be increased.**

Now, the question becomes, is the spoken word limited to an atmosphere of air such that sound waves must carry the vibrations? Consider the table[14] below that lists the Hebrew alphabet and the reference to the sounds as provided by the International Phonetic Alphabet (IPA).

Illustrative words

IPA	Letter	Example			IPA	Letter	Example		
/p/	פ	/ˈpe/	פה	'mouth'	/b/	ב	/ˈben/	בן	'son'
/m/	מ	/ma/	מה	'what'					
/f/	פ	/oˈfe/	אופה	'baker'	/v/	ב, ו	/ˈnevel/	נבל	'harp'
/t/	ת, ט	/ˈtan/	תן	'jackal'	/d/	ד	/ˈdelek/	דלק	'fuel'
/ts/	צ	/ˈtsi/	צי	'fleet'					
/s/	ס, ש	/ˈsof/	סוף	'end'	/z/	ז	/ze/	זה	'this'
/n/	נ	/ˈnes/	נס	'miracle'	/l/	ל	/ˈlo/	לא	'no'
/tʃ/	צ׳, תש	/tʃuˈka/	תשוקה	'passion'	/dʒ/	ג׳	/dʒiˈrafa/	ג׳ירפה	'giraffe'
/ʃ/	ש	/ʃaˈna/	שנה	'year'	/ʒ/	ז׳[1]	/ˈbeʒ/	בז׳	'beige'
/j/	י	/ˈjom/	יום	'day'	/w/	ו	/ˈpiŋgwin/	פינגווין	'penguin'
/k/	כ, ק	/ˈkol/	כל	'all'	/g/	ג	/gam/	גם	'also'
/x/	כ, ח	/ex/	איך	'how'	/r/	ר	/ˈroʃ/	ראש	'head'
/ħ/	ח	/ˈħam/	חם	'hot'	/ʕ/	ע	/ʕim/	עם	'with'
/ʔ/	א, ע	/reʔaˈjon/	ראיון	'interview'	/h/	ה	/ˈhed/	הד	'echo'

Fig. 21.1 Hebrew phonetic alphabet compared with corresponding IPA phonetics

Voice recognition software has come to the forefront. Linguists call the various sounds phonemes and these form an integral part of voice recognition software. The number of phonemes used vary from language to language. Some of the recent English programs use 44 phonemes. Phonemes are used in cross-language translations—sort of a machine version of the day of Pentecost technology.

The question is often asked as to what the really original spoken word looked like? Of course, there are so many voices, opinions and controversies that one might think highly degreed and pedigreed Bible scholars have beaten their pens into swords for weapons to use against each other. However, in a larger sense, we owe a great debt to those who have transcribed and translated the word of God tirelessly over the years. We don't know what the original word really was, but we do know that as we seek the Spirit of God the truth will eventually be revealed and all mankind will marvel at the truth that has been hidden from the foundation of the world.

Some have seen the Hebrew characters as dancing letters of fire. One viewpoint is that the original language was all verb based and constructed around three letter root words. These root words, if understood, provide the underlying spiritual meaning of the quickened motion and creative flow of the Spirit. This is a strange concept to western thought and to most languages today. Perhaps, there is a QVV—a Quickened Verb Version somewhere in the spiritual realm.

Why should we spend time digging through ancient scriptures when eventually the Spirit of God will reveal it to us anyway? Perhaps, part of the reason is the many skeptics say the Bible is full of myths and half-truths. Consider the shock and surprise that will be experienced when it is being revealed that scientific principles were encoded into the scriptures from the beginning. Then, mankind will be reconciled back to God.

2 PETER 3:9 The Lord is not slack concerning his promise, as some men count slackness; but is longsuffering to us-ward, **not willing that any should perish, but that all should come to repentance.**

Is there a time coming, when we will no longer need the pressure waves of air to hear one another. Will we communicate across great distances because time and distance in the spirit is not the same as the natural realm?

1 CORINTHIANS 15:40 There are also celestial bodies, and bodies terrestrial: but **the glory of the celestial is one, and the glory of the terrestrial is another**.
41 There is one glory of the sun, and another glory of the moon, and another glory of the stars: for one star differeth from another star in glory.

2 CORINTHIANS 3:17 Now the Lord is that Spirit: and where the Spirit of the Lord is, there is liberty.
18 But we all, with open face beholding as in a glass the glory of the Lord, are **changed into the same image from glory to glory, even as by the Spirit of the Lord.**

We all look forward to the day when no longer will we need our terrestrial ears to hear the spoken word. But—in a very natural way—we will speak to each other in what is now considered telepathic language. Will our celestial eye see the dancing letters of fire in the Spirit?

For this mortal body will put on immortality and death will be swallowed up in victory!

22 SUMMARIZING THE PATTERNS

We have explored the land of Bible acrostics in detail. Now, let us take flight as an eagle and look back over the path we have traveled. Here are our chapter notes.

CHAPTER 1 *If We Could Only Witness Creation's Beginning*

The concept was proposed that the discoveries of science are not new technology but were well-known by God as part of the creation of the world. The concept given in Hebrews was discussed that worlds were framed by the word of God so the seen things were brought forth from the unseen. Fundamental to the beginning of creation is light: **Let there be light.** Words involve alphabetical characters and since the Old Testament was written in Hebrew, it is highly probable that Hebrew characters and words were used to frame creation. The general structure and pattern of acrostics was introduced with this contemporary example.

Apples are a tasty fruit.
Bees pollinate flowers.
Camels travel the deserts.
Doors often have locks.

CHAPTER 2 *From Darkness into Light*

The seven lamped Hebrew candlestick stood in the tabernacle as a symbol of light. For creation began with the phrase: Let there be light. The configuration of the candlestick was quite unique in that a total of twenty-two almond buds were engraved within its lamp stems. There are twenty-two letters in the Hebrew alphabet and most likely these letters were embedded in the creative linguistics as God spoke creation into being. Both sound and light are 'waves' and come in set of eight—for example octaves on a piano.

The master key of Hebrew letters and patterns is given in Psalm 119. For each of the twenty-two letters of the Hebrew alphabet, there is a set of eight verses which begin with the Hebrew letter for that set.

CHAPTER 3 *A Rod of an Almond Tree*

This chapter is a follow-up of the twenty-almond buds on the seven lamped candlestick of light. It traces the almond rod as the symbol of God's power of the spoken word. The Bible tells us that this rod was used by Moses in Egypt, for parting of the Red Sea and for many miracles in the wilderness of Sinai. How do we know this was an almond rod? Moses and brother Aaron were of the tribe of Levi and the scriptures tell us Aaron's rod bloomed almonds.

CHAPTER FOUR *Scientists "Discover" Seven Hidden Dimensions*

This chapter introduces recent discoveries by scientists of hidden dimensions in the unseen world. It is said that in addition to the four seen dimensions (length, width, depth and time) there are total of seven unseen dimensions. The question is asked if the seven lamped candlestick is symbolic of the Seven Spirits of God—for the Spirit of God did hover over the dark waters in the beginning.

The relationship between the twenty-almond buds (twenty-two Hebrew characters) and the seven lamps was explored. The number of 3.14… and the fraction 22/7 or 3.14… are nearly, but not quite identical. The Pi unending series of numbers was explored for multiples of eleven, such as 22, 33, 44, etc.

The world of fractals was introduced—which is a way that nature reproduces itself in a cookie cutter fashion. It's configuration was compared to the candlestick in the way it seems little candlesticks (fractals) are growing out the larger candlesticks. The escape iterations of growth for a daughter fractal to reach an 'escape velocity' from its mother fractal was related to eleven when a multiple of Pi is reached. A simple feedback equation for the fractal cycles was introduced: $Z_{(n+1)} \longrightarrow Z_n^2 + C.$

CHAPTER FIVE *The Acrostic Pattern for DNA*

The patterns for DNA and RNA (protein builders) were presented. There are twenty-two letters in the Hebrew alphabet and twenty-two autosomes. We get twenty-two autosomes from our mother and an additional twenty-two from our mother. This along with the 23rd sex determining chromosome from our mother plus the 23rd sex determining chromosome from our father make up the forty-six total human chromosomes.

CHAPTER SIX *The DNA and RNA Codes*

The structures in the DNA spiral were examined. The chemical names for the cross-links on the DNA ladder were shown in simplified form as the A—T and the G—C relationships. An example was given of how the DNA 'library' is opened up so that a messenger strand of the RNA protein builder can receive the code for constructing the many proteins utilized in our body.

CHAPTER SEVEN *The Twenty-two Letter Protein Building Code*

This chapter further illustrated the protein building process and presented the IUPAC RNA table which gives the codes for assembly. This code has twenty-two positions with a START at the eleven position and a STOP at the twenty-two position.

CHAPTER EIGHT *Chromosomes and Genes*

An overview of a cell containing a nucleus containing a chromosome having a DNA spiral ladder is presented. The huge number of cells within the human body—in excess of ten trillion—each have a huge library of information within the DNA in the nucleus. It took thirteen years for scientist to work their way through decoding the human DNA—imagine that same library in over ten trillion cells. This chapter then delved into each of the twenty-three chromosomes and their estimated 21,000 builder genes. The diseases that could result from defects in the first chromosome was presented.

The relationship between the Hebrew numbering system and variables such as Pi and the natural logarithm base e were discussed in detail. Plotting the Hebrew numbering system using a logarithm function shows a series with repeating nodes at multiples of eleven—similar to the START/STOP in the DNA/RNA codes also in the iterations for a daughter fractal to be fully formed and escape from its mother.

The multiples of eleven in both the Pi and the base e series were examined and two short equations were presented for these processes.

CHAPTER NINE *Acrostics in Proverbs, Psalms and Lamentations*

The Psalm 119 acrostic does not stand alone in the Bible. There are more acrostics in Psalms, Proverbs, Lamentations, Esther and Nahum. These are discussed along with quotations showing what other Christian writers have written about acrostics. The Proverbs chapter 31 acrostic is examined in detail as a pattern of a complete acrostic. The Hebrew characters their corresponding numbers are also presented.

CHAPTER 10 The Roots of the Hebrew Language

This chapter explores what we would consider strange in a language—the absence of vowels. It discusses the beginnings of language as revealed in secular archaeological studies as well as the language written by the finger of God on the two tablets of the ten commandments.

CHAPTER 11 *The Body of Christ Working Together*

Moses and King David were given specific plans for the construction of the tabernacle/temple. David was required to detail this in writing. But, we know the true temple is the human body and we are fearfully and wonderfully made. This chapter presented the invitation for the body of Christ to work together to uncover the nuggets of gold hidden within the texts of the acrostics and examine their relationship to creation.

CHAPTER 12 THROUGH CHAPTER 21 *Detailed Presentation of Bible Acrostics*

These chapters provide the Hebrew and English texts for the numerous Bible acrostics. We have tried to format these such that our readers will be able to readily discern the form and fashion of the acrostic patterns.

CHAPTER 22 AND THE APPENDIX
Summarizing the Patterns plus Treasures of Science in the Bible

The Appendix details treasures of science contained in the Bible and was recommended for those readers that might be initially skeptic about the Bible even having a scientific basis.

Chapter 22 (this chapter) is a summary of the road we have traveled. King David wrote many of the Psalms and many of the acrostics—and was also given the blueprint for the temple. He was a talented musician playing on a harp of ten strings. Ten strings plus the harp framework holding the strings is an eleven dimensional musical instrument.

PSALM 49:4 I will incline mine ear to a **parable**: I will open my dark saying upon the **harp**.

PSALM 144:9 I will sing a new song unto thee, O God: upon a psaltery **and an instrument of ten strings will I sing praises unto thee.**
10 It is he that giveth salvation unto kings: who delivereth David his servant from the hurtful sword.

This king was skilled in music and in writing—perhaps he was given songs of the universe—some of which have purposely been hidden in the acrostics. The acrostics are like a parable and when we dig deeper the dim form of "something there" is brought to light.

We would like to conclude this book with comments made by Michio Kaku, a professor at City College of New York. Dr. Kaku participated in the Science Channel program ***Parallel Universes*** that we discussed in chapter 4 of this book. He has his own weekly radio show and is a well-known science commentator for the TV networks. You may remember his statement as being somewhat prophetic about looking down from the mountain.

In a video which has gone viral—Dr. Kaku discusses the eleventh dimension, the mind of God and the music of strings resonating through hyperspace. You may watch the video at this internet link.:   http://bigthink.com/dr-kakus-universe/math-is-the-mind-of-god (accessed 7/7/2016).

This video includes a discussion of the interplay of agreement and tensions between scientists and mathematicians over the years and how some of these have been resolved—an example being super string theory. Dr. Kaku has stated his belief that we live in a world made by rules and by an intelligence. Text from his video message seemed a fitting way to end this book.

" It turns out that 100 years ago, math and physics parted ways. In fact, when Einstein proposed special relativity in 1905, that was also around the time of the birth of topology, the topology of hyper-dimensional objects, spheres in 10, 11, 12, 26, …

"Well, physics plodded along for many decades. We worked out atomic bombs. We worked out stars. We worked out laser beams, but recently we discovered string theory, and string theory exists in 10 and 11 dimensional hyperspace. Not only that, but these dimensions are super. They're super symmetric. A new kind of numbers that mathematicians never talked about evolved within string theory. That's how we call it 'super string theory.' Well, the mathematicians were floored. They were shocked because all of a sudden out of physics came new mathematics, super numbers, super topology, super differential geometry."

"All of a sudden we had super symmetric theories coming out of physics that then revolutionized mathematics, and so the goal of physics we believe is to find an equation perhaps no more than one inch long which will allow us to unify all the forces of nature and allow us to read the mind of God. And what is the key to that one inch equation? Super symmetry, a symmetry that comes out of physics, not mathematics, and has shocked the world of mathematics. But you see, all this is pure mathematics and so the final resolution could be that God is a mathematician. And when you read the mind of God, we actually have a candidate for the mind of God. The mind of God we believe is cosmic music, the music of strings resonating through 11 dimensional hyperspace. That is the mind of God."

****

APPENDIX

TREASURES OF SCIENCE IN THE BIBLE

Is the Bible just another ancient book full of myths and scientifically flawed, or does it contain concepts that modern scientists are just 'discovering now? We will present some scientific gems from the Bible for your consideration.

How Could Job's 3500 B.C. Description of the Earth Match a Modern Astronaut's View from Space?

Fig. A.1   Photo: Earth from Space – Courtesy of NASA

How could what modern astronauts are seeing from space and what is written in the ancient book of Job perfectly coincide? The short answer for Christians was given by the Apostle Peter when he wrote: *For the prophecy came not in old time by the will of man: but holy men of God spake as they were moved by the Holy Ghost.* To be concise, the scriptures were written as their hand was directed by God and God should know because He created the earth.

YES, THE WORLD HAS MANY SKEPTICS ABOUT THE SCRIPTURES—but it totally confounds them to try to explain how Job could have precisely described an earth **hanging from nothing in space**, **circular** in nature and having a **visible dividing line** between day and night.

The adventurous among us eagerly look forward to the day when we can become space tourists and see the earth suspended from nothing. Consider the reaction of Apollo 12 Astronaut Alan Bean's as chronicled in a 2012 Science Channel presentation entitled NASA's Unexplained Files. He made these comments about the launch and his first impressions of the earth from space:

> "The thought that ran through my head was, 'I hope the metal in this space ship is strong enough to withstand the vibration. It is more than I ever imagined that machinery could stand and still operate. *I looked for the wire that is holding this earth up for a second.* You can't suddenly change from an earthling to a spaceling.'"

DID JOB WRITE THE SAME THING AS MODERN ASTRONAUTS HAVE OBSERVED?

JOB 26:7 He stretcheth out the north over the empty place, and **hangeth the earth upon nothing**.
8 He **bindeth up the waters in his thick clouds**; and the cloud is not rent under them.
9 He holdeth back the face of his throne, and spreadeth his cloud upon it.
10 He hath **compassed the waters with bounds, until the day and night come to an end**.

From his observations about the earth **hanging from nothing**, the waters **compassing** the earth in a circular fashion and the view of **the day-night dividing line**, Job was certainly far advanced beyond his 'flat earth' contemporaries.

THE EARTH'S MAGNETOSPHERE AND THE SOLAR HELIPAUSE

Theories about the solar plasma stream and its interaction with Earth were published as early as 1931. During the next several decades multiple scientists, including Sydney Chapman and Hannes Alfvén, proposed a variety of mechanisms and explanations. The Earth's magnetosphere was first measured in 1958 by Explorer 1 during the research performed for the International Geophysical Year.

Fig. A.2 Artist's Rendition of the Earth's magnetosphere[15] (Courtesy NASA)
https://en.wikipedia.org/wiki/File:Magnetosphere_rendition.jpg (accessed July 12, 2016)

PSALM 47:9 The princes of the people are gathered together, even the people of the God of Abraham: **for the shields of the earth belong unto God**: he is greatly exalted.

Ever wonder why the astronauts wear the reflective face shields in space or when on the moon? It is to protect them from the radiation particles from the sun. The magnetosphere does just that for us on earth so that we don't have to walk around with shielding in our normal everyday life.

Until recently, scientists have theorized about an interstellar boundary where the solar wind from the sun meets the galactic wind from the universe. The voyager space explorer recently reached what is thought to be the interface area where very harmful galactic radiation is stalled by the solar wind from the sun. Consider this scripture:

PSALM 84:11 **For the LORD God is a sun and shield**: the LORD will give grace and glory: no good thing will he withhold from them that walk uprightly.

The scriptures not only describe a shield for the earth but show that the sun—the source of harmful radiation—is also a shield, not only for the earth but for the other planets within the interior solar system.

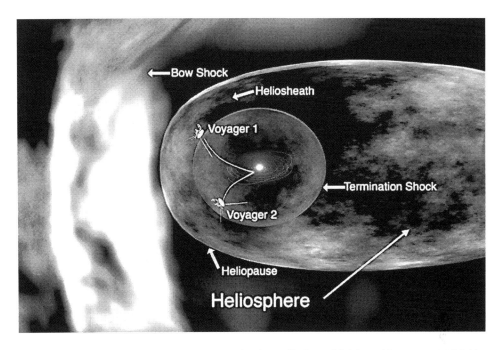

Fig. A.3 The 'bow' shock of our sun's galactic radiation shield [16] (Courtesy NASA)
http://science.nasa.gov/media/medialibrary/2009/12/22/23dec_voyager_resources/heliosphere_big.jpg

The above illustration shows the sun (on the left hand side) and then the planets until a region is reached where the solar wind from the sun shields us from the galactic radiation.

THE FOUR WINDS

Scientists have in relatively modern time 'discovered' the four winds. The four winds are also referenced in the Bible and we are finding that these winds are much more than just a figure of speech.

MATTHEW 24:31 And he shall send his angels with a great sound of a trumpet, and they shall gather together his elect **from the four winds, from one end of heaven to the other.**

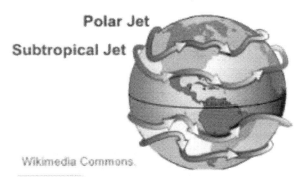

Fig. A.4 The four jet streams[17] Wikipedia.org, s.v. "File: Jetstreamconfig.jpg" http://en.wikipedia.org/wiki/File:Jetstreamconfig.jpg (accessed June 20, 2013).

As we have watched recent weather patterns, we have become quite aware of the effects of these jet streams upon our ambient temperatures. **Polar vortexes** have become part of the everyday vocabulary of the general public.

DO MORE ADVANCED CIVILIZATIONS EXIST IN THE GALAXIES?

Nikolai Kardashev of the former Soviet Union was a pioneer in the Soviet part of the SETI program to search for extra-terrestrial intelligence. He theorized that given the very large number of galaxies in our known universe, super civilizations might exist which are far more advanced than our earth civilization. He even went so far as to develop a classification system for superior civilizations that we might ultimately encounter. I think he had three classes of so-called superior civilizations.

A synopsis of Kardashev's civilizations classification was summarized by Michio Kaku in chapter 13 of his book *Hyperspace*:

> Futurology, or the prediction of the future from reasonable scientific judgments, is a risky science. Some would not even call it a science at all, but something that more resembles hocus pocus or witchcraft. Futurology has deservedly earned this unsavory reputation because every "scientific" poll conducted by futurologists about the next decade has proved too wildly off the mark. What makes futurology such a primitive science is that our brains think linearly, while knowledge progresses exponentially....
>
> With all these important caveats, let us determine when a civilization (either our own or possibly one in outer space) may attain the ability to master the tenth dimension. Astronomer Nikolai Kardashev of the former Soviet Union once categorized future civilizations in the following way....
>
> The basis of this classification is rather simple: Each level is categorized on the basis of the power source that energizes the civilization. Type I civilizations use the power of an entire planet. Type II civilizations use the power of an entire star. Type III civilizations use the power of an entire galaxy. This classification ignores any predictions concerning the detailed nature of future civilizations (which are bound to be wrong) and instead focuses on aspects that can reasonably be understood by the law of physics, such as energy supply.
>
> Our civilization, by contrast, can be categorized as a Type 0 civilization, one that is just beginning to tap planetary resources, but does not have the technology and resources to control them. A Type 0 civilization like ours derives its energy from fossil fuels like oil and coal, and, in much of the Third World, from raw human labor. Our largest computers cannot even predict the weather, let alone control it. Viewed from this larger perspective, we as a civilization are like a newborn infant.

****

Given the billions and billions of stars and planets, many scientists will theorize that it is likely that civilizations much more advanced than earth's exist out there somewhere.

What do you believe?

If you believe that a civilization more advanced than earth exists, have you considered that the leader of that more advanced civilization might be God?

PSALM 19:1 **The heavens declare the glory of God; and the firmament sheweth his handywork.**

REFERENCE NOTES

Citations following are presented here with the understanding that it may not necessarily follow that the authors are in overall agreement with the themes presented in this book.

CHAPTER FOUR

[1] *The World of π*, David Boll in 1991. (http://www.pi314.net/eng/mandelbrot.php accessed 7/2/2016)

CHAPTER 5

[2] BiblicalHebrew.com, "Alphabet," http://biblicalhebrew.com/alphabet.htm (accessed 6/22/16)

[3] RNA codon table showing four sets of four or 64 codons total
https://en.wikipedia.org/wiki/Genetic_code#RNA_codon_table (accessed 7/8/2016)

CHAPTER 6

[4] A fluorescence micrograph of a cell during metaphase of mitosis.
Credit: DR PAUL ANDREWS, UNIVERSITY OF DUNDEE/Science Photo Library/Getty Images
http://biology.about.com/od/mitosisglossary/g/spindle_fibers.htm (accessed 7/7/2016)

CHAPTER 7

[5] CODON RNA BUILDING ILLUSTRATION
https://en.wikipedia.org/wiki/Genetic_code (accessed 7/4/2016) TransControl; mRNA; CC BY-SA 3.0; File:RNA-codons.png; Created: 12:13, 22 May 2007 (UTC)

[6] **Inverse table (compressed using IUPAC notation) at website**
https://en.wikipedia.org/wiki/DNA_codon_table (accessed 7/4/2016)

CHAPTER 8

[7] CELL TO CHROMOSOME DIAGRAM
https://en.wikipedia.org/wiki/Chromosome#/media/File:Eukaryote_DNA-en.svg
(accessed 7/4/2016) DNA in Eukaryote cell; 5 August 2012; Derived from file Eukaryote DNA.svg; Author: Eukaryote_DNA.svg: *Difference_DNA_RNA-EN.svg: *Difference_DNA_RNA-DE.svg: Sponk (talk)translation: Sponk (talk)Chromosome.svg: *derivative work: Tryphon (talk) Chromosome-upright.png: Original version: Magnus Manske, this version with uprightchromosome: User:Dietzel65Animal_cell_structure_en.svg: LadyofHats (Mariana Ruiz)

[8] TABULATION OF BASE PAIRS FOR GENES
https://en.wikipedia.org/wiki/Chromosome; Human chromosomes section of article; (accessed 6/24/2016) Partial table from Sanger Institute's human genome information in the Vertebrate Genome Annotation (VEGA) database)

[9] CHROMOSOME 1 DISEASES AND DISORDERS
https://en.wikipedia.org/wiki/Chromosome_1_(human)#Diseases_and_disorders (accessed 7/72016)

[10] PBS HUNTING HIDDEN DIMENSIONS ILLUSTRATION
http://www.pbs.org/wgbh/nova/physics/hunting-hidden-dimension.html (accessed 7/4/2016]

CHAPTER 9

[11] J.A. MOTYER ACROSTIC INFORMATION
http://www.bible-researcher.com/acrostics.html (accessed 7/7/2016)

[12] Hebrew Alphabetic Acrostics – Significance and Translation; ROELIE VAN DER SPUY; NORTH WEST UNIVERSITY, SOUTH AFRICA AND SIL INTERNATIONAL; *ABSTRACT:* Van der Spuy: Hebrew Alphabetic Acrostics *OTE* 21/2 (2008), 513-532 513

CHAPTER 19

[13] *Mysterious Noncoding DNA: 'Junk' or Genetic Power Player?* from an email by Jenny Marder, November 7, 2011 at 4:03 PM EDT from this website (accessed 6/30/2016) http://www.pbs.org/newshour/rundown/junk-dna/

CHAPTER 21

[14] https://en.wikipedia.org/wiki/Modern_Hebrew_phonology (accessed 7/28/2016)

APPENDIX

[15] EARTH'S MAGNETOSPHERE (Courtesy NASA)
https://en.wikipedia.org/wiki/File:Magnetosphere_rendition.jpg
(accessed July 12, 2016)

[16] BOW SHOCK ILLUSTRATION; Courtesy NASA;
http://science.nasa.gov/media/medialibrary/2009/12/22/23dec_voyager_resources/heliosphere_big.jpg

[17] THE FOUR JET STREAMS Wikipedia.org, s.v. "File: Jetstreamconfig.jpg" http://en.wikipedia.org/ wiki/File:Jetstreamconfig.jpg (accessed June 20, 2013).

Made in the USA
Lexington, KY
22 April 2017